Praise for the Books of

Michael Ian Black

"[*Navel Gazing* is] funny and sad and ridiculous and searching and humane and the gravitas sneaks up on you, and the last page had me in tears."

—Elizabeth Gilbert, author of *Eat, Pray, Love*

"Set him on the recommended shelf beside Sedaris and Fey."

—*Booklist*

"Dear Michael Ian Black: please stop writing things in books that I wish I had written myself, it's starting to make me feel bad."

—Samantha Bee, host of *Full Frontal with Samantha Bee*

"I loved *My Custom Van*. But I loved *You're Not Doing It Right* even more . . . Touching, hilarious, and truthful all at once. What else do you want, America?"

—Mike Birbiglia, author of *Sleepwalk with Me*

"Michael Ian Black is one of the finest comedy minds of our generation and a master at assembling words in a hilariously pleasing way."

—Chris Hardwick, of *The Nerdist*

"Michael Ian Black has proven that even the most simple-minded among us can occasionally create works of genius."

—Stephen Colbert on *My Custom Van*

"Solid, sensitive, and often appropriately silly . . . Unlike many other books by comedians, this memoir never feels like a series of onstage routines transcribed to make a buck."

—*Publishers Weekly* on *Navel Gazing*

ALSO BY MICHAEL IAN BLACK

You're Not Doing It Right

My Custom Van

America, You Sexy Bitch (with Meghan McCain)

NAVEL GAZING

True Tales of Bodies, Mostly Mine

(but also my mom's, which I know sounds weird)

Michael Ian Black

GALLERY BOOKS

New York London Toronto Sydney New Delhi

G

Gallery Books
An Imprint of Simon & Schuster, Inc.
1230 Avenue of the Americas
New York, NY 10020

First Gallery Books trade paperback edition August 2017

GALLERY BOOKS and colophon are registered trademarks of Simon & Schuster,
Inc.

For information about special discounts for bulk purchases, please contact Simon &
Schuster Special Sales at 1-866-506-1949 or business@simonandschuster.com.

The Simon & Schuster Speakers Bureau can bring authors to your live event.
For more information or to book an event contact the Simon & Schuster Speakers
Bureau at 1-866-248-3049 or visit our website at www.simonspeakers.com.

Interior design by Akasha Archer

Manufactured in the United States of America

10 9 8 7 6 5 4 3 2 1

Library of Congress Cataloging-in-Publication Data for the hardcover edition is available.

ISBN 978-1-4767-4883-2
ISBN 978-1-4767-4882-5 (hardcover)
ISBN 978-1-4767-4884-9 (ebook)

For my family

If I ever leave this world alive
I'll thank you for the things you did in my life
If I ever leave this world alive
I'll come back down and sit beside your
Feet tonight
Wherever I am, you'll always be
More than just a memory
If I ever leave this world alive

—Flogging Molly, "If I Ever Leave This World Alive"

NAVEL GAZING

Introduction

"Oh shit," you may think, "I am going to die"

My mother has no belly button. They took it during one of her "major" surgeries. Over the last fifteen years or so, Mom has had so many surgeries, she now divides them into categories to keep them straight in her head. Minor surgeries are the outpatient ones, like when she visits the specialist who refills the deck-of-cards-size pain pump implanted in her side. Major surgeries are those requiring extended hospitalization and recovery, like the several surgeries she has had to cut away evermore inches of dead intestine, or the time they returned her appendix to its home below her abdomen from where they found it floating near her lung as if it were a lost cat. The bellybuttonectomy was part of a major surgery to untangle an intestine that had looped itself through her bowel, a potentially fatal condition.

Before the operation, her doctor asked Mom how attached she felt to her navel, explaining that if she felt the need to preserve it, a plastic surgeon could be brought in to tie together a new one for her like a balloon knot. If a doctor ever asks me how attached I am to my own belly button, I will answer "Very!" because although I am not crazy about any of my body parts, I am selfish enough that I would like to keep them all.

Mom told the doctor she did not hold her own belly button quite so dear. "Good," he said, since the plastic surgeon would require an additional expense not covered by whichever insurance company had the misfortune to hold my mother's policy. It's hard to argue with an insurance company refusing to pay for a new navel. Even I, a proponent of universal health care and renowned hater of The Man, would have a hard time defending the expense of reconstructive belly button surgery. So, with Mom's blessing, they took it. Where her belly button used to be, there is now just skin, like a pothole that's been paved over.

How strange to not have a belly button. After all, a belly button is one of those things that define us, not only as humans, but as members of the entire biological class *Mammalia*. Without a belly button, you could just as easily be fish or fungus. Having it taken seems like a peculiar kind of bodily transgression, as if a burglar broke into your house but only stole your high school ring.

Growing up, I don't remember Mom ever having so much as a cold, despite the fact that she struggled with her weight her entire life, never exercised, and spent years smoking Virginia Slims, the feminist cigarette. Then, almost overnight, it all turned to shit.

Her health woes began in a teeny vacation cottage she once owned in the Blue Ridge Mountains with her partner, Sandy. They used to spend a month there each summer after Sandy's term as a South Florida preschool director ended. The cottage is where Mom first noticed persistent and heavy bleeding from her lady parts. (As her son, I am incapable of writing anything more specific than "lady parts" when describing my mother's lady parts.)

The telephone calls to me and my brother, Eric, were brief and to the point: She had uterine cancer. . . . They'd found it early, Stage 1. . . . Her prognosis was excellent. . . . No, she didn't need us to fly down there. . . . She and Sandy would be returning to Florida for surgery, followed by a course of radiation. . . . We should go about our lives as if nothing were amiss. . . . Updates forthcoming.

Cancer is a scary diagnosis, of course, but Mom did not seem worried. Or perhaps she chose to keep the worry from her words so as not to alarm us. And perhaps we let her do this because, even though we are adults, we are also still her children, and children, no matter how old, allow themselves to be gullible with their parents, because being gullible is often easier than being wise.

Upon her return to Florida, Mom underwent a radical hysterectomy. The surgery revealed bad news. Her cancer had invaded the uterine wall, escalating her diagnosis from Stage 1 to Stage 3. Cancer diagnoses are divided into four stages, with Stage 4 being terminal. They are further subdivided into letters *a* through *c*. Mom's cancer was rediagnosed as Stage 3c, one squiggly letter away from a death sentence.

A few years ago, I wrote a book called *You're Not Doing It Right*, a (very good, please purchase) memoir about romantic relationships and marriage. This book is a follow-up, focusing on time and family and the body—subjects I began thinking about with a certain degree of seriousness around the time Mom first got sick, and deepening after I turned forty. Forty is that moment most of us believe ourselves to be balanced right at the fulcrum of the life-expectancy teeterboard. On one side, we see our parents' generation starting to get old, some of them sick, some already dead. On the other, our children's generation, brimming with a vibrant joie de vivre best described as "annoying." And there you are, balanced between the two for a split second before beginning your inexorable slide toward the land of dashed dreams and broken hips and assisted living facilities and death.

Once you hit forty, it is no longer possible to pretend you will remain forever young. In fact, according to the Social Security Administration, a man like me, age forty-three, only can expect to live an additional thirty-eight years. In other words, I am already past my life's midpoint; calling myself middle-aged is, at best, a fudge, at worst a disservice to the entire field of mathematics. Even so, I don't feel like my life is more than halfway over. I feel exactly as I did ten or fifteen years ago. Yet somehow whole decades have elapsed in the time I've spent upgrading my iPhones through their various iterations. Entire species have gone extinct as I drove around the mall looking for better parking spaces. Then one day, I look up and a government agency is informing me I am no longer a zesty young man, but a just-past-middle-aged adult with adult responsibilities and a mortgage and the first signs of erectile dysfunction. This moment eventually happens to all of us, the moment when you first sense that the road you are traveling may, at some point, end. And when that realization hits, it does so in the sudden, jarring manner of a car crash: "Oh, shit!" you may think at the moment of impact. "I'm going to die."

No doubt some people shrug their shoulders at this revelation. Not me. I panicked. My reaction, I suspect, is the more common of the two. In fact, vast swaths of the economy exist precisely to serve as a balm for this midlife hysteria. The sports car industry. The cosmetic surgery industry. The divorce industry, and its attendant trophy wife industry. Youth may be wasted on the young, but billions are wasted on the middle-aged.

My panic catalyzed a thorough examination of my place in the universe, starting with my body. For most of my life, I'd thought about my body only in terms of how best to endure its inadequacies. I'd never done a thorough head-to-toe review of my corporeal self. Yes, I'd had physicals, but those only served to provide raw data points. Such-and-such blood pressure, such-and-such cholesterol, such-and-such this, that, and the other thing. All of which could be weighed and sorted and inputted onto spreadsheets to be distributed among interested medical practitioners and members of

Obama Death Panels. And when I began this process of thinking about myself from a physical perspective, as opposed to a more mental or creative perspective, I discovered something that sent me into a psychic tailspin, something that made my mother's cancer seem insignificant. What I discovered is this: I was losing my hair.

Not a lot. Not enough that other people would necessarily even notice. Certainly not so much that I couldn't disguise it through artful arrangement. But how long before "artful arrangement" metastasized into comb-over, the hair loss equivalent of a Stage 3c diagnosis?

I'd managed to go through the first forty years of my life with no discernible hair loss, and now, just as I'm confronting my own mortality, I start to go bald? How about one thing at a time? I don't consider myself a particularly vain man, but that is only because I am lying. The truth is, I am incredibly vain, even though I have very little to be vain about. But I do have a full head of hair. At least I did. Now I have most of a full head of hair, but also an increasingly visible scalp, and a swirly patch at the back of my head, a plain once lush as the Serengeti, but which grows more parched and drought-stricken by the day, and threatens to erode into a full-blown bald spot. Well, not on my watch, hair. Not on my watch.

I researched male-pattern baldness. I bought volumizing shampoos. I learned esoteric terms like *DHT*, a chemical derivative of testosterone that, when imbalanced, miniaturizes the hair follicles. I read up on hair transplants, even going so far as to ask my accountant if I could deduct such a procedure as a business expense. (He said I could, since I am an actor, and actors must have thick, glossy manes, except for Bruce Willis, who can do whatever he wants.) Finally, I made an appointment with a New York hair-restoration specialist, who, to my surprise, turned out to be the single baldest man I have ever seen. He looked like a condom with eyes.

My appointment lasted less than ten minutes. He ran a portable microscope over my scalp, beaming images of all my lovely, individual follicles onto a small television monitor. Yes, he could definitely see thinning, but I still had too much hair to qualify for a transplant. Instead, he prescribed finasteride (Propecia) pills and topical minoxidil (Rogaine), both of which I will have to use for as long as I wish to retain my lustrous locks, which is forever. Even after I am dead.

Obviously, I'm joking about comparing hair loss to my mom's cancer. Nobody should get too worked up about something as superficial as thinning hair. Except I did. Because hair loss is only superficial when it happens to somebody else. When it happened to me, it felt cataclysmic. That doctor's waiting room was like a funeral home, filled with somber guys in various states of mourning. Some, like me, appeared more or less hirsute. Others, in more advanced stages of grief, wore baseball caps or pushed their remaining hair forward to camouflage their emerging foreheads, or sported full beards to distract from their lack of topside locks. If hair loss is no big deal, what were we all doing there? And why did we refuse to look each other in the eye? I'd visited intensive care units more upbeat than this place. Why? Because everybody is guilty of catastrophizing the trivial, especially when it comes to our bodies. I know this is true, because were it not, we would not have coined the word *cankle*.

The great writer Nora Ephron titled her final essay collection *I Feel Bad About My Neck*, as apt a description of this condition as any there's likely to be. Personally, I never felt bad about Nora Ephron's neck, but I certainly feel bad about the leukemia that killed her. Apparently, Nora didn't speak much about her cancer, preferring to keep her large sufferings private, her small ones public. It is an impulse I understand well. Funny people do not want pity. They want laughs. And money. (Mostly money.) I hope Nora Ephron at least made peace with her neck before she died. Who wants to go to the grave feeling bad about her neck? Or thighs or stomach? Feet, yes. Feeling bad about one's feet is understandable.

I feel bad about my feet.

Here are some other things I feel bad about: the almost 1:1 ratio of the diameter of my upper arms to my wrists; the red blob on my chest, which I am told is a harmless blood vessel, but which reads to the untrained eye like a little clown nose; the fact that my mustache grows at a much quicker rate than my beard, so that I have the perpetual look of a thirteen-year-old Mexican boy; the fact that my right shoulder rests higher than my left no matter how many times throughout the day I attempt to rearrange my spine; my height, which is two inches less than optimal; the curvature of my nose, which is approaching Owen Wilson levels of unsightliness; my drooping scrotum, which, by the year, is slowly sinking into the earth like the city of Venice; the mysterious red slashes I discover on my shoulders and back each morning, the result of "sleep scratching," which, after researching, I discover is an actual *mental disorder* I seem to have, as is my trichotillomania, the compulsive desire to pull out hair—in my case, beard whiskers—resulting in a large bare patch under my right jawline where there should be beard, which does nothing to diminish my thirteen-year-old-Mexican-boy look. I feel bad about my escalating weight and the amount of arm hair I have, as well as my armpit hair, which extends farther down the underside of my arm than I think it ought to, and also the shade of my skin, which is the Crayola color between "pallid" and "jaundiced." This is only a partial list.

On the other hand, there are things about which I feel pretty good. My health, to this point, has been excellent, although it is hard to convince myself it will remain so if I continue to eat, as I did last night after everybody had gone to bed: half a bag of Tostitos, a bowl of ice cream, more Tostitos, and three stale almond cookies that tasted fine once I brushed the dog hair off them. Moreover, I am sixteen years into a marriage, a marriage I expect to last *at least* another six weeks. We have two kids who do not yet hate us. Plus, although I am gaining weight, I am still thinner than almost all of the guys I went to high school with, which is the only metric that matters. Also, since I am often unemployed, I get plenty of healthful sleep. My sexual engine, never a dynamo, continues to putter along at the libidinous equivalent of a Toyota Camry, decent and workmanlike, but not setting any performance records. And then there is my belly button. It is a fine belly button, an innie, chockablock with small kernels of linty debris and dead skin, a veritable cornucopia of buried treasure. Were I ever to lose my navel, I would surely miss it.

Mom's updated cancer diagnosis demanded a new, more aggressive treatment. In addition to the standard course of external radiation she'd already agreed to, the doctors now proposed adding internal radiation, a process where a team threads a radioactive cocktail of cesium, iridium, and iodine into the patient through a catheter, using advanced imaging technology to position the pill as near to the cancer as they can get it. Once that is achieved, they run away because the patient is now, literally, radioactive. I'm not exaggerating. Patients undergoing internal radiation therapy are quarantined in a "hot room" for three days while the body absorbs the poisonous fissile material. It's like eating a nuke. During those three days, patients are not allowed visitors, and medical staff provide care from a distance. I asked Mom how she got her food. "They threw it," she said.

(I also ask the obvious question, but the answer is no: Despite being inundated with mysterious radioactive material, she acquired no superpowers.)

The radiation therapy was painless, but being alone for three days drove my normally voluble mother batty. She passed the time reading, watching TV, and twirling her bra above her head like a lasso. At the end of her quarantine, the medical staff used a Geiger counter to ensure her body was no longer shooting off death beams.

Upon checking her torso, they discovered Mom had written florid messages of thanks all over her stomach in Magic Marker. Everybody had a good laugh, and they sent her home. She checked out of the hospital, spirits high. "Great," she thought. "That's the end of it."

But her troubles had just begun.

CHAPTER ONE

Loud and embarrassingly ethnic

I'm running. It's mid-March here in the wilds of Connecticut, where I live, and I'm running through snow in boots that reach to my calves, and I am lost. I've been in the woods about an hour attempting, without luck, to tire out our new white Labrador puppy, Ole. (Named for my wife Martha's great-grandfather and pronounced in the Norwegian manner, "O-lee," not like the Spanish, "O-lay.") Ole and I started on the blue trail, but somewhere along the way, the blue trail turned into the white trail, and now I don't see any trail markings at all. The sun is starting to close up shop for the day, and I am running, not out of any anxiety about making it home before dark, but because running in snow, even while wearing thick and clompy boots, feels great.

The dog stays behind me, sometimes at my heels, sometimes hundreds of yards back as he investigates the smells of other animals, nibbling on their feces as if sampling various hors d'oeuvres at a party being thrown in his honor. When I lose sight of the dog for too long, I stop and yodel, "Ole Ole Ole!" After a moment or two, I see his big dumb head poking up from the bramble. He catches my eye and bounds to me through the snow, tail whirling like a boat propeller. I take off at a trot again, peering through the woods for a trail. There is none. I have the sun to my left so my general direction must be north. Or is it south? This is exactly what you get when your mother won't let you join the Boy Scouts because it's a "sexist organization."

I talked to Mom this morning. Her health is stable for the moment. Not great. Not even good. It will never be good again. But stable. As a result, our regular phone chats no longer begin with her latest health calamity. Over the past few years of such talks, I have become more familiar with the technical shortcomings of various colostomy bags than I would have ever believed possible, this despite the fact that never once have I opened a conversation with my mother by saying, "Please, tell me about your stoma."

She no longer walks, relying on a motorized scooter to get around the microscopic apartment she rarely leaves other than for doctors' appointments. Sandy still works full-time; she would like to retire, but Mom's medical expenses have made that impossible. So Mom is alone most of each day except for her own dog, a barky bit of fluff named Jake. When I visit, Mom instructs the dog to "say hello to your brother," meaning me. I would prefer she not do this.

We usually talk about once a week. We talk about books and the weather and my work. She asks after the grandkids. Sometimes they get on the phone and tell her about their various doings. Elijah, fourteen, has to be prodded to say anything. Ruthie, eleven, has to be prodded to let anybody else say anything. Sometimes when Mom and I get on the phone, neither of us has much to say at all, so we cut it short. But every phone call ends the same way:

"Love you, Mikey."

"Love you, too, Mom."

When somebody you love has a chronic illness, you get used to living with a prickly, low-grade fear. Unpleasant thoughts are always hovering, like a housefly that won't be swatted. For a time, I can forget about the fear, but then the phone buzzes at ten o'clock at night and my first thought is always of Mom.

People used to tell me I was Mom's spitting image. We share the same hair color and skin tone and hazel eyes and full lips. I liked looking like her because it made me feel that I fit somewhere. When Martha and I talk to our own kids about which of us they most resemble, I see in their eyes the same eagerness to know where they belong. Sometimes we pretend to argue about who got whose nose or chin. Now that they're getting older, though, they're beginning to look less like us and more like each other. They look like they belong to the same family and sometimes it startles me to realize it's *my* family.

I never knew most of my relatives. When he was alive, Dad wasn't close with anybody in his family other than his sister Jane. Mom's family mostly resided in Chicago, whereas Dad's work had exiled us to suburban New Jersey. Sometimes Mom told stories about growing up enveloped in a thick cloud of aunts and uncles and cousins. But the names—Anna and Mollie and Lefty—meant nothing to me. Even the idea of "family" seemed kind of fuzzy. Whatever understanding I had of families I gleaned from television commercials, which tended to portray them as large groups of overweight people arguing in accented English about who made the best tomato sauce. Families seemed loud and embarrassingly ethnic. I didn't think I needed one.

I knew a little bit about my family, of course, including the fact that I am named for a mobster, which is, by far, the coolest thing about me. Although he is long dead, I will refer to this man as "Uncle Mobby" because his relatives are still very much alive and I do not wish to be sued or killed.

Uncle Mobby was the husband of my great-grandaunt who, by the time I knew her, was an ancient and tiny woman living alone in an elegant Chicago high-rise. The apartment reeked of old-lady smells: potpourri, lemony furniture polish, wet perfume. I liked visiting her because she kept small crystal bowls filled with silky chocolates, protection money in exchange for not destroying her home. Also, she kept an extravagant yellow windup bird in a brass birdcage hung from the ceiling. Every so often she would wind the bird for us. Out came lovely canary song, its yellow-feathered head swiveling, wings flapping. Then it would fall silent again and we would be left to wonder at its hidden workings. According to my mother, this aunt possessed fabulous wealth. With candies and windup birds like that, I didn't doubt it.

Uncle Mobby never wielded a tommy gun. Never shook anybody down. Never garroted a rat with piano wire. His participation in Chicago's Prohibition-era Jewish mafia, or "Kosher Nostra," was more subdued. Mobby was a money launderer, one of the green-visor guys who "wash" ill-gotten gains through various legitimate businesses so that it may safely be recirculated back into the square world, to be spent on Buicks and chinchilla coats and pinkie rings. One of my uncle's legitimate businesses was an actual Laundromat, which I suppose is a pretty good joke if you are a mobster.

He died not long before I was born, and Mom gave me his first initial—M for "Mobby"—as a way of honoring her aunt's many kindnesses to her throughout her life. The aunt is gone now, too, as is their only child, a boy named Bert who followed his father into the family business.

When I found Bert's obituary online, it contained loving words of remembrance about his family and charitable deeds, but mentioned no occupation. I tried to unearth more information about him, finally discovering a corporation he founded in 1980, which named him as vice president and secretary, and his wife as president. As far as I could tell, this company conducted no business activities during the three decades of its existence. It just sat there in a kind of corporate vegetative state. Of course, corporate inactivity doesn't necessarily imply anything nefarious. I have a company, too, and to the untrained observer it would appear that mostly what I do, as president and CEO, is spend hours a day surfing Twitter. Such an assumption would be insulting, and the fact that it's correct makes it all the more offensive.

The Mobbys are my family's only outlaws. I count no cattle rustlers among our clan. No international drug kingpins, diamond smugglers, or brilliant forgers of art. Instead, my ancestors were an ordinary assemblage of Ukrainian immigrants fleeing religious persecution. In the nineteenth century, Tsar Alexander III passed a series of regulations, known as the May Laws, that restricted the amount of property Jews could own and where they could live. Revisions to the laws over the years prevented Jews from becoming doctors and lawyers, attending universities and high schools, and, eventually, from participating in elections. It was as if Tsar Alexander III decided that Jews would experience all of Russia the same way Kevin Bacon experienced that terrible town in *Footloose*.

Millions fled, including my great-great-grandfather Philip. He came to America in 1894 with his second wife, Rose, and nine kids. Rose and Philip had three more children in America, and probably would have kept going had she not done him the great discourtesy of dying. That left Grandpa Philip in a strange country with no wife and twelve children. Twelve. I can't even imagine. Martha and I only have two, and we needed a battalion of au pairs to survive.

The family settled in Chicago, where Philip picked up his old job as an "egg candler," an old-timey term for somebody who inspects fertilized eggs, a job originally performed with the aid of candlelight. His sons followed him into the produce business. Eleven of the twelve eventually married and had children of their own. Most stayed in Chicago, although a few scattered to Texas and California and New Jersey. One married a money launderer for the mob.

Many of the men served in the armed forces: I have seen their draft registration cards online. There is my great-great-grandfather Philip, age forty-one, registered to serve in the First World War. The cards of various great-uncles registered for the second. Some went to war, and some died. One, a navigator during World War II, received a posthumous Silver Star for sacrificing his own life helping his crewmates escape after their plane was shot down over Austria. My mom's father, Sam, served in the navy during World War II. I ask Mom if he saw combat. She laughs. In a war that took millions of lives and upended continents, my grandfather found himself stationed in Rio de Janeiro. The closest he got to battle was having an anchor tattooed on his forearm.

After the war, Grandpa Sam came home and married my grandmother Cecile. He became a salesman, selling restaurant franchises across the country. For years, the family scraped by, but toward the end of his life, he began making what my mom calls "good money" from a fried-chicken restaurant. After years of struggle, the American dream finally seemed at hand. Although Grandpa was overweight, his health appeared good, his ever-expanding stomach the by-product and just reward for a life well lived.

One day, my mom received a call from her father telling her not to be nervous, but he was at the hospital, having just been rammed from behind in a minor car accident. The doctors wanted to keep him there for observation, he said, and he would be home in a few hours. He never left. While conducting routine tests, the doctors discovered a huge mass. It was the mass, not the fried chicken, making his stomach grow. They tried, but there wasn't much they could do.

Now it's Mom's turn to deal with cancer, or in her case, its aftereffects. Now I am the anxious child concerned for his parent, and Mom is the one reassuring me not to worry, she'll be fine, but she also likes to remind me in a half-joking way that she is dying. If I neglect to call her often enough, for example, she'll say, "Why don't you call more? Don't you know I'm dying?" It's an effective tactic.

Mom says she wants to be cremated when she dies, her ashes placed in "a *very* fancy box." Me too. I don't like the idea of being stuck in a coffin and lowered into the ground. What if I'm not really dead? Better to get burnt up than buried alive. Sandy wants a proper burial, though, so they've decided that after they're both gone, Mom's ashes will be placed in Sandy's casket. They've already picked out their plot, discounted because Sandy works at the synagogue.

I ask Mom if I can have her leftover oxycodone when she dies.

"Sure," she says. "Although now that I'm on the pain pump I don't get prescribed the good stuff."

"I'll take the pain pump then."

She agrees to leave me the pain pump.

I'd always assumed that chronically ill people grow to accept death, the way Martha eventually grew to accept the Portuguese foreign exchange student who shared her bedroom with her when she was fifteen. It wasn't something she'd asked for, but after ignoring the girl, then fighting with her, she eventually grew to accept this unwelcome guest. I ask Mom if death scares her, expecting her to tell me that, no, she may have been at one point, but now she has learned to accept it.

"I'm petrified. Not even scared—petrified."

So there goes my theory about death being like a Portuguese foreign exchange student.

"Why?" I ask. Maybe this is a dumb question. Maybe it's obvious why somebody would be petrified of dying, but Mom's day-to-day attitude is so good that I have a hard time reconciling her fear with the way she lives her life. I guess I expect her to answer that she's petrified because, duh, death is scary for everybody, or that she's, duh, worried about pain, or that, duh, she's scared because she doesn't know what's going to happen next. But I don't expect the answer she gives.

"Because I don't feel like I did anything with my life."

Oh.

That kind of takes the fun out of the conversation we were just having about her imminent demise. My first instinct is to feel offended. Didn't do anything with her life? She had *me*, a very attractive man.

When I press her, she says she feels like she squandered her potential, that she hasn't made "a contribution." Death petrifies her because her time is short and now she feels she never will.

I understand. Most of us want to leave the world having secured some sort of legacy through our works and deeds. But it strikes me as such a futile idea—that we should be *remembered* at all. Remembered by whom? Do we expect unborn generations to sing our praises? If so, why? What's the best any of us can hope for, anyway—that some future sixth grader will one day write a book report about us? As the parent of a sixth grader, I can assure you they are lazy researchers and terrible writers.

Personally, I feel no great need to be remembered, except by my kids and, hopefully one day, grandkids. And when I do die, I don't want any pomp. I want to be cremated, my ashes flushed down the nearest toilet. In lieu of a funeral, I would like a party held in my honor featuring buffalo wings and Hanson's "MMMbop" playing on a loop. That's enough. Besides, now that Maya Angelou is dead, who would speak at my memorial?

I tried telling Mom all of this, that the best contribution any of us can make is to be there for each other, the way Mom was there for me and Eric and our younger sister, Susan. The way I try to be for Elijah and Ruthie. Our legacies aren't our own, anyway, I don't think. I think they're all bound together with those of the generations that came before and those of the new ones ahead. I'm named for my uncle the mobster, and I carry him around with a certain amount of wicked pride, just like I carry around the legacy of an egg candler who raised twelve kids without a single Swedish nanny, and my grandpa who spent the war at Carnival. Just like I carry around all my great-aunts gathered in a Chicago kitchen arguing in accented English over who makes the best potato pancakes. I tried explaining all this to Mom, but the words didn't come out right, or maybe she just doesn't see it the same way.

Last night at dinner, Elijah said he believes in ghosts. "That's because you're an idiot," I thought, although I refrained from saying so. Thinking about it today, though, I realized I do, too. Not the spooky kind. Not the tormented souls that rattle chains and draw out their vowels when speaking. The ghosts I believe in are more earthly than that. They don't do any scary shit. In fact, they don't do much of anything at all. Mostly, my ghosts just sit around a beat-up card table, smoking cigarettes, drinking old cans of Meister Brau. They tell stories, and their stories tell me who I am.

It's almost dinnertime again and I'm still out on the trail with the inexhaustible Ole. The big dummy looks at me like I know where I'm going. I don't. I'm just out here sliding along on the snow and ice. But then, up ahead, I spot a blue rectangle spray-painted on a tree trunk. The trail marker. We follow it through the woods toward home.

CHAPTER TWO

"That explains why you look like that," she said

One of the unfortunate by-products of conducting genealogical research is cataloguing all the various and sundry ways in which one's relatives met their ends. Here be congestive heart failure. Here be polio. Here be industrial accidents and lightning strikes and diseases of the spleen. Each ancestor's death is like a fun-house mirror asking, "Will you too be felled by the French pox?"

Yes, medical advances have lessened my odds of contracting the plagues of yore, but I hold no faith in living a long and fruitful life. From my earliest days, I have been conditioned to accept the fact that my time here on earth is apt to be brief and horrid. Because I have bad genes.

We can escape lions and we can escape fire, but we cannot escape our DNA. We are who our ancestors were. Every day, the newspapers are filled with stories of centenarians crediting their longevity to "food, fun, and hard work" or "faith in God." I even just read about a Texas woman who believes drinking three cans of Dr Pepper a day has sustained her for a hundred and four years. But the truth is, if you want to live a hundred years or more, none of these things will help you very much. What you need, more than anything, are the right genes. Biology is destiny. Which is how I already know I am not going to live to be a hundred. Or even ninety. Eighty is, at best, an iffy proposition. I'll probably make it to seventy considering Mom has, and she's basically being held together with Silly Putty at this point.

The poor quality of my family genes was an oft-discussed topic in our household while I was growing up. On what felt like a nightly basis, Mom would remind me and Eric that our medical futures looked bleak, her words delivered with the weary resignation of a tarot reader who'd just flipped over the Death card.

I knew my genes to be bad despite all evidence to the contrary: I am of normal height and weight and have never contracted any serious illness. My good cholesterol is good, and my bad cholesterol is also good. Blood pressure fine. Eyes serviceable enough. And most importantly, my back is naturally hairless. Were I to roll these attributes while creating a Dungeons & Dragons character, I would have said the gods had favored me. Yet I remain convinced that I am, at best, moments from a horrific death.

Cancer runs thick and greasy through my family blood, and the odds are good that one day I will wake up with a tumor growing off me like a clump of poison sumac. The only real mystery is which kind of cancer I'll get. Mom had uterine cancer, which I think I am safe from due to my lack of having a uterus. But I've also heard tales of bone cancer, lung cancer, and prostate cancer scattered across my lineal terrain like so many IEDs. My family's real bogeyman, though, is colon cancer. In a bit of grim familial symmetry, my father's mother and mother's father both died from it. From the time I first gained awareness of my own asshole, Mom has been encouraging me to have it explored. "Get a colonoscopy when you are forty," she would say, a procedure that, now age forty-three, I have yet to undergo. My brother got one, though, and he's fine, so I probably don't need to, since the laws of genetics dictate that whatever is up his butt must also be up my own.

Yet despite Mom's relentless fearmongering, it never occurred to me to question whether or not my genes are, in fact, "bad." Why would I? I found confirmation everywhere I cared to look. My grandparents' early cancer deaths constituted a potent piece of evidence. So did Eric's cleft palate, with which he was born, necessitating several childhood surgeries. Plus, our sister Susan has Down syndrome. (I learned later that her form of Downs, trisomy 21, is not genetic, but I didn't know that while growing up.) Besides, even had I chosen to find out more about my genes, until recently it wasn't possible to do so. Scientists could peer into the deepest reaches of space and read the story of the universe, but our own genetic code remained indecipherable alphabet soup. That changed in 2003 when a team of biologists, geneticists, and computer scientists first decoded the human genome.

Since then, genetic testing has advanced so quickly, and the price fallen so much, I was able to go online and order a kit for ninety-nine dollars that accomplishes much of what it took thousands of scientists and cost a billion dollars to discover just over a decade ago.

Instead of reading the entire genome like goddamned show-offs, companies like the one I ordered my test from use a process called genotyping, which compares markers in an individual's DNA to reference markers in control DNA. It works like one of those "What's wrong with this picture" games they have in *Highlights for Children* magazine, with computers matching your genome against a control genome. The discrepancies between the two are genetic abnormalities that can be linked to your specific health risks. I also ordered a kit for Martha, reasoning that she, too, would enjoy knowing which disease will one day kill her.

"I'm not doing that," she says when the tests arrive.

"But don't you want to know if you're going to get something?"

"No."

"But . . . but . . ." I have no good argument to present her other than that I paid almost a hundred bucks for the kit, not the most persuasive tactic when trying to convince somebody to learn if she will one day develop Alzheimer's.

The "would you rather know or not know" question is one of those increasingly common dilemmas with which all of us must wrestle. On the one hand, knowing may give us the kick in the pants we need to take preventative measures. On the other, what good is knowing if there is nothing that can be done, especially because genetic testing rarely gives binary yes/no answers, offering instead a range of likely outcomes? Just because you have the BRCA1 or BRCA2 genes does not mean you will definitely get breast cancer, although it greatly increases your odds. Angelina Jolie, for example, discovered herself to be a BRCA1 carrier and lopped off her breasts via a preventative double mastectomy. Perhaps that was a sound decision, but she also carried a vial of Billy Bob Thornton's blood in a locket around her neck when they were married, so I think it's fair to question her judgment.

Martha's attitude does not dissuade me from opening my own test box. I'm not sure what I expect to find inside, but I assume there will be an assortment of science gizmos including: a hypodermic needle, a high-speed centrifuge, a DNA sequencer, safety goggles, and a tabletop laser. Not so. The box contains exactly one (1) plastic spittoon and one (1) mail-in envelope. I shake out the box, but that's it. Hm. Shouldn't the process for untangling my personal double helix be a bit more *Star Trek*y than filling a plastic cup with spit?

It takes ten minutes of effortful expectorating to fill the cup. When I finish, I hold it up to the light, the way schoolkids do conducting experiments on pond water. Somewhere in that watery goop is my fate. I seal up the envelope and mail it off to the future.

A couple weeks later, I receive an e-mail informing me that my results are ready for viewing. On the website, I find a tremendous amount of information broken down into four categories: "Health

Risks," "Drug Response," "Inherited Conditions," and "Neanderthal Ancestry." Whoa, whoa, whoa. Neanderthal ancestry? Everything else would now have to wait. Nothing is—or ever could be —more important than finding out my Neanderthal ancestry.

Here's the deal: I am 2.9 percent Neanderthal. That may not sound like a lot, but it is a full .2 percent above the norm. In other words, I am nearly 10 percent more Neanderthal than the average person! This was the manliest thing that had happened to me since getting hit in the eye with a pitch during Little League. For somebody as insecure about his masculinity as myself, learning I am basically a full-blooded Neanderthal felt incredible. My overabundant arm hair, which I'd always found vaguely embarrassing, now seemed primal and raw. Erotic, even. I rush to tell Martha the good news.

"I'm a Neanderthal!" I tell her, showing off my test results. I expect her to whip off her clothes and start humping me then and there.

"That explains why you look like that," she said.

"Like what?"

"You have a Neanderthal brow."

She's right. I do have a heavy brow. It overhangs the rest of my skull like a buzzard on a tree limb. How did she manage to transform my cool genetic idiosyncrasy into a jab about my physical appearance? Damn her and her more highly evolved *Homo sapiens* brain. Well, the joke's on her—she's the idiot who married me.

Deflated, I return to the website, turning to my lines of ancestry, which are a total letdown. As it happens, I am exactly what I have always believed myself to be: 100 percent Ashkenazi Jew. The Ashkenazi branch of Judaism is characterized by our European roots, our long history traced to the original Israeli tribes, and our love for National Public Radio. It did surprise me to learn that we Ashkenazis are considered our own distinct ethnicity, owing to the fact that there has been so little marrying outside the faith over the last five hundred years (which, I'm sorry, is a little gross). In fact, according to Wikipedia, I am genetically more similar to an Ethiopian Jew than I am to a European gentile.

No ethnic wild cards exist in my lineage. No Native American or East African or Pacific Islander. This is disappointing. I would like to be at least a *little* Maori. But no. I am a bland mélange of Eastern European shtetl dwellers. I'm borscht. At least my kids have a tastier genetic makeup because I had the good sense to marry a Viking.

Martha is a tall Minnesotan blonde, a statuesque descendant of Norwegians and Irishmen, with a sprinkling of Luxembourgian thrown in as genetic bling. Or so she claims. Until she spits into the cup, I don't trust a word she says. *If* her ethnic claims are one day confirmed, it will mean our two kids are a rich brew of nearly the entire European continent minus Italy, which is just as well, because the Italians are savages.

Next, I turn my attention to the subject I have been dreading: "Health Risks." Clicking the link, I expect to find a giant blinking nuclear hazard symbol informing me that I am already dead. Instead, the page lists a long column of diseases, along with my approximate odds of contracting each.

The disease I am most likely to develop is not, as I believed, colon cancer, but something called "atrial fibrillation," which I learn is basically an irregular heartbeat. That doesn't sound like a big deal. I mean, how bad can an irregular heartbeat be? If you're going to be at high risk for something, it might as well be for something as innocuous as a heart that looks bad on the dance floor. Out of an abundance of caution, I do a little more research into the matter. Big mistake. Although the Mayo Clinic website assures me that "episodes of atrial fibrillation can come and go" without too much cause for concern, the American Heart Association wants me to know that "AF" can lead to "stroke, clotting, heart failure, and death." Death does not sound good. Stupid heart.

I am also three times more likely than the general population to develop "venous thromboembolism," which is a fancy way of saying blood clots. As it happens, I already knew this, because my aunt nearly died from a venous thromboembolism of her own. Had she not admitted herself to an emergency room after experiencing persistent pain in her leg over the course of several days, her doctors said, she likely would have been dead within twenty-four hours. After her scare, she contacted Eric and me to get tested. I scheduled an appointment and got the test. It came back positive, now confirmed by my DNA test. Stupid clots.

My doctor said there isn't much I can do about it other than take a daily baby aspirin, get exercise, and make sure I walk around when flying long distances, all of which I now do, except for the part about getting up and walking around when I fly, and exercising.

Some other stuff I am at elevated risk for: gallstones, chronic kidney disease, rheumatoid arthritis, macular degeneration, and, most distressingly, lung cancer. Lung cancer??? My lung cancer number is legitimately scary: 11.6 percent. That's a lot of percent. How can it be that high? I have never used any tobacco products. I don't smoke cigarettes or cigars or pipes or chew tobacco, although I do confess to thinking that hookahs look kind of cool. Can admiring hookahs elevate my risk of lung cancer?

Panicked, I take an online "lung cancer risk test" that asks me a bunch of questions, primarily about my smoking history (none), whether I have ever worked with asbestos (no), and if any work I do or have done with mustard gas was performed with adequate protection (yes, all of my mustard gas work was done with adequate protection). After I submit my answers, the test informs me I have a "much below average" risk of contracting lung cancer. Further research tells me the genetic component of lung cancer is far less of an indicator than environmental factors. Phew. Mentally, I adjust my odds of getting lung cancer from the 11.6 percent figure to 0.0

percent, because of all the medical strategies known to mankind, denial is the most effective.

But wait—where is colon cancer? I'm supposed to get colon cancer. Mom said so. Nowhere on my "elevated health risk" list does it mention anything about colon cancer.

After working my way through the elevated-risk column, I explore my "decreased risk" section, where I learn I am at lower risk than the general population for contracting, among other things, prostate cancer. That's good news. After all, the prostate and the colon are physically very close to each other. I think they may even share a cubicle. If I'm at decreased risk for one, I must be at decreased risk for the other.

The last list is "average risk," where I finally find my colon and rectum. Despite a lifetime of dark portents from my mother, it turns out I am almost exactly average in terms of risk for colorectal cancer. Average risk! This is a huge relief. My colon is run-of-the-mill. Boring, even. It's the kind of colon you wouldn't even look twice at if you passed it on the street. All those years of worry for nothing. Well, not nothing. I mean, I do have an average risk for colorectal cancer, which is 5.6 percent. But still, that's a considerable reduction from total certainty. Bad genes, my ass. Or, more precisely, average genes: my ass.

I'm going to live forever! I celebrate my good news by not getting a colonoscopy.

A few months after receiving my test results, I read a newspaper article saying the Food and Drug Administration has forbidden my genetic testing company from continuing to sell their product, expressing concerns about the "validity of their results." How can that be? The validity of their results is the only thing separating them from a company that sells overpriced spittoons. Maybe everything they told me is a lie. Maybe my genes really are bad. Maybe I am right back where I started, fretting about the future, convinced of my own imminent demise. Maybe, but I'm not going back to worrying about that stuff. I can't. It's too exhausting. I'll just do what I can do. I will get my colon checked out—soon, I promise. I will continue taking my daily baby aspirin. I will also continue taking my hair medication, which has nothing to do with any of this, but I thought it prudent to reassure readers of this book that my hair will always look cool. But one thing I will no longer do is get freaked out over a future I cannot control. Because I am a Neanderthal. And we Neanderthals Do. Not. Give. A. Fuck.

CHAPTER THREE

What they are thinking is this: "Dad sucks"

A few months after her time-out in the hot room, Mom returned to the oncologist for a routine follow-up. It was supposed to be a quick howdy-do and a lollipop on the way out. Instead, he found a mass right near the area where her cancer had been. "A *big* mass," Mom emphasizes to me.

The doctor didn't mince words. "I'm really sorry," he said, "but I don't see any way that it's not terminal."

One day in the distant future, when I receive my own death sentence, I like to think I will accept the news with solemn grace. I like to think I will nod once or twice, take a moment to gaze out the window at this good, green earth, then rise to shake the doctor's hand. In a vaguely British accent, I will tell him not to feel too bad, old boy, it's been a good show. Then I will spin on my heel and take my leave, fading into nothing as he bangs his fist against his desk shouting, "Damn it! Damn it all to hell!"

That's not how Mom took it. She says she felt like she'd been punched in the stomach. She says she felt terrified and angry and hopeless. Her doctor said they would do what they could, which is, of course, what they always say. It's what they'd told her father years before. The oncologist made plans to remove the growth. Maybe they could get enough of it that they could start chemo. Maybe they would get lucky. Maybe. But he made it clear to Mom that he didn't think so. In the meantime, he instructed Mom to "get her affairs in order," a phrase I didn't think existed outside of movies. Mom staggered from his office, ordered her affairs, and prepared to die.

And that's where the story gets a little weird.

A week or so later, as Mom and Sandy drove to the hospital on the morning of her surgery, Mom heard a voice. Or maybe it would be more accurate to say she heard A Voice, deep and male, the kind of 1950s Paramount Pictures voice that once commanded Charlton Heston to part the Red Sea. Like Moses, she alone heard the Voice, which delivered its message unto her and departed as inexplicably as it had come, taking with it the terror she'd felt since receiving her diagnosis, leaving in its place an abiding calm.

She turned to Sandy. "I just heard a voice," she said. "I don't know if it was God or who it was, but the Voice told me the tumor isn't malignant."

Sandy's reaction was basically, "Whatever you say, Jill."

Mom had her surgery. Afterward, the doctor entered her recovery room with news: To his shock, the tumor had turned out to be benign. Mom thanked him for the update but tells me she didn't feel surprised. She'd already known.

This is exactly the kind of story I would normally dismiss out of hand when told to me by somebody else. *Yeah, yeah, you heard a voice. Go play with a crystal.* But it's harder to do that when the person involved is your mother. I know her to be a rational person and, aside from her love of country music, a person with reasonable mental faculties. She'd never heard voices before, never communicated with the Great Beyond, never professed any great spiritual fervor. After Susan was born with Down syndrome, my mother even dropped her belief in God. Not because of Susan's health issues, but because the rabbi refused to conduct a naming ceremony in the temple for a child with mental retardation. So Mom didn't seem to be the most likely candidate for otherworldly intervention. Yet, when it happened, she accepted the event with a strange nonchalance, relating the story to me with the indifference of somebody describing an unspectacular episode of *The Good Wife*. I can't decide if her blasé attitude indicates a healthy, open mind or a complete psychotic break. I know that my reaction would have been considerably different. First, I would have torn off all my clothes and run into traffic. Then I would have sought out the only spiritual advisor that matters, but who knows if Oprah would even take my call?

My own spiritual problems are profound. I don't believe in God but I also don't *don't* believe in God. The usual term for people like me is *agnostic*, but I hate that word because it gives people an intellectual dodge, a way to feel smug about their own ignorance: "Well, I can't prove there is a God, but of course, I can't prove there *isn't* a God, either." Well, la-dee-dah for you, smart guy. But a paradox isn't a philosophy.

Better to take a stand. Better to know what one believes. Except I have no idea, finding myself caught between wanting to believe in God but unable to allow myself to do so. I'm a devout believer born into the body of an atheist. There is no word for people like me, so I made one up: *praytheist*, which I define as, "Somebody who prays to a god in which he doesn't believe, hoping to find evidence for God's existence, which, if found, he will then dismiss."

It was easy enough to keep my spiritual struggles to myself until we had kids. But Martha is Catholic, and once we found ourselves in possession of a couple of pliable minds to mold, she wanted to send them to Sunday school. I objected for reasons I had a tough time articulating.

"I don't want to do that," I said when she broached the idea.

"Why not?"

I had hoped just me saying I didn't want to do that would have settled the matter, since I wasn't prepared to actually defend my position with, you know, *reasons*. Again, my wife was outmaneuvering me with that damned *Homo sapiens* brain of hers. But even old *Homo neanderthalensis* can occasionally pull a card from his sleeve. "Because I'm not Catholic."

Game. Set. Match.

She responded that she *was* Catholic, and that since I was not a practicing Jew, she didn't understand why I should mind the kids learning about her religion. Moreover, she would not object if I *also* wanted to send them for Jewish instruction. I told her I didn't see why they needed any religious education whatsoever. Again, she wanted to know why not. But this time, I had my answer prepared.

"Because I don't want them to."

My argument, such as it was, boiled down to this: Why should we force-feed our kids some made-up story as truth just because their mom was brought up with that story, a story she's not even sure she believes; and also, isn't it better to let our children arrive at their own conclusions about religion in their own good time instead of giving them answers to questions they haven't yet even thought to ask; and also, shouldn't their father's gnashing existential angst/low-grade chronic depression serve as a shining example of how to conduct one's spiritual life?

Martha's response boiled down to this: because I want to, no, and no.

After months of back-and-forth, I finally relented, for two reasons. The first is because giving them some religious training was ultimately more important to Martha than not giving it to them was to me. But the second, far more important reason, was that she volunteered to get up early and drive them every week, which, honestly, constituted most of my objection to the idea in the first place.

So each Sunday, the kids trooped off to Catholic class, where they colored and filled out biblical worksheets and sang about Jesus loving them, this they know. After a couple years, their formal religious education concluded with a confirmation ceremony involving two hundred dollars' worth of new clothes they would never wear again. Ruthie had to don a creepy white veil, which I guess signified a holy union with the Church, but which veered uncomfortably close to child-bride territory for my taste.

All in all, harmless enough, but I don't think Jesus really worked his way into their open and trusting hearts. Now that Sunday school has ended, they don't talk much about God, or pray, or do any of the Jesus-y things I would expect from true believers. For example, neither has ever offered to wash my feet or tithed to me their birthday money. The kids do sometimes attend church with Martha, but when I ask them what they got from the service, what they most often mention are the free doughnuts.

A couple times they have asked me if I believe in God. My instinct is to dodge the question the way I used to when they asked whether Santa is real. "Do *you* think Santa is real?" I would parrot to them, which, for some reason, provoked their feeble little brains into muddled silence. Unfortunately, their intellects have now matured enough that they demand real answers to real questions. But I have no answers. I have nothing to offer them. A father should not appear to be a flailing idiot in front of his children. Yet when it comes to matters of faith, a flailing idiot is what I am. So rather than trying to skirt the issue in the hope of preserving their naïve faith, I go with the truth.

"I don't know what to believe," I tell them. "I think the world is a beautiful place and I think there is a lot of love in the world. Did God create the world and the love? A lot of people think so, but personally I don't know."

It's the best answer I can give, but I can see in their eyes that they

want something more definitive. Because I am their father, sometimes I can read their thoughts. This is one of those times, and what
they are thinking is this: "Dad sucks."

They're right. I do suck. But it's not my fault. All blame for my
spiritual shortcomings rests with my parents. They are the ones who
raised me without religion, so it is only natural that I am faithless.
Mom only allowed herself to grow reacquainted with Judaism as
part of her courtship with Sandy, a devout Jew. They attended synagogue together, shared Shabbat dinners with Sandy's friends, and,
together, discovered new and terrible Jewish music.

When it finally reawakened after decades in hibernation, Mom's
Judaism expressed itself with the fierce righteousness of the once
were lost but now are found. For a while, she threatened to cross
the dividing line between regular Jew and Super Jew, even doing
that cute thing moms do where they throw a tearful fit about their
son's Catholic wedding ceremony not including any Judaic tradi-
tions even though she raised that son without religion and the son
never even set foot in an actual temple other than to attend other
people's bar mitzvahs so it seemed a touch odd to her son that she
should get so upset about it and certainly not worth throwing a hissy
fit over in front of the priest her son had reluctantly agreed to allow
to officiate to appease his fiancée and almost ruining the wedding
for everybody. Cute mom stuff like that.

Thankfully, Mom soon burned off most of her white-hot religi-
osity. Now it just kind of burbles away at a low simmer. She sends
cards and Hanukkah gifts and five-dollar bills to the kids during the
High Holidays but she doesn't push it on me or them. Honestly, it's
nice. The kids know they are half Jewish, although they would be
hard-pressed to explain what that means, since I don't really know
what being Jewish means, other than the happy fact that I control
the media.

Somehow for Mom, receiving an unexpected supernatural message fit into her worldview. When it came, she never questioned its validity. A voice (or "Voice") told her the tumor was benign, and so it was and so it ever shall be. End of story. I envy her. Were it me, I would be forever turning over the events in my mind, trying to convince myself that what I knew had happened didn't actually occur.

I ask Mom if she ever heard the Voice again. She says yes, one other time.

"Really?! What did it say?"

"I can't remember," she responds.

"You can't remember?"

"I really can't."

How do you not remember what a voice—a voice you believe might be the actual voice of God—tells you? I am not the most conscientious listener, but when a prophetic voice starts whispering the secrets of the universe in my ear, at the very least, I jot the message down on a Post-it note. You know, just in case I forget what it said. WHICH I WOULDN'T DO! I mean, I met Dan Aykroyd twenty years ago and I can remember every word of *that* conversation, but my mom can't remember what God Almighty told her? What if it was the secret to world peace? Or, more importantly, what if it was about me? I have not been this angry at my mother since she convinced me to get a perm in sixth grade. She promises to tell me what it said if she ever remembers. Thanks, Mom.

CHAPTER FOUR

Too good to be true

Although I can't quite bring myself to believe in God, I pretty much believe in everything else. I'm willing to entertain any crank theory about UFOs, the authorship of William Shakespeare's plays, fluoride in the water, the Bermuda Triangle, Bigfoot, black helicopters, false flag operations, and Star Children. You say Lee Harvey Oswald was the patsy in a Russian/Cuban/CIA/mafia conspiracy? I believe it. You say Lee Harvey Oswald acted alone? I believe it. At any given moment, the conviction I hold most dear is whichever thing is the last one I heard. Yet even I—gullible idiot that I am—know that when a telephone rings and a man on the other end tells you a long-lost uncle has died and left you money, that man is a liar. So when I received such a call several years ago at my office, I said to the man, "You, sir, are a liar."

Everybody knows that long-lost uncles are not a real thing. They may have been at one time, perhaps in the days of Charles Dickens, when people were routinely shanghaied from cobblestone streets and disappeared onto pirate ships, never to be heard from again. Back then, everybody had a long-lost uncle, or at least a misplaced cousin or two. But long-lost uncles are not a thing now. Not when we have GPS and the NSA. Nobody's uncles are ever "lost." They are either at home building model railroad sets or in jail for touching their nieces.

Besides, the idea that a relative of mine would leave behind any kind of worthwhile estate was ridiculous. Other than my gangland namesake, my family has never had much money. If they had, it either would have been squandered on dubious business opportunities or invested with Bernie Madoff or something. To die with more assets than liabilities is as exotic a concept to my family as crunking.

When I called the man on the phone a liar, he sighed. "That's what everybody says when I call, but it's true. You have a great-uncle on your father's side who recently died." He then detailed a fair amount of information to me about myself and my family, and told me he would be sending me a form so I could claim my inheritance.

"How much money is it?" I asked. I didn't mean to be indelicate about the subject, but etiquette seemed unimportant while discussing fictional sums.

"I can't say," the man told me. Did that mean he didn't know or he wasn't allowed to say? He told me he didn't know, that his job was to locate the estate's heirs, which he had now done. Click.

After hanging up, I told my coworkers about the call. They agreed it sounded like a load of hooey. Worse, it wasn't even persuasive hooey. Long-lost uncle. Please. This was amateur hour. This was "You wanna buy the Brooklyn Bridge?"–level bad. Of course, I *wanted* to believe the guy. Who wouldn't want to believe such a thing? I am a huge fan of receiving money for doing nothing; it's the main reason I became an actor. But this was too good to be true.

Later that night, I told Martha about the call. "That sounds too good to be true," she said.

"I know."

"But what if it is true?"

"How could it be true?"

"I don't know," she said. "How much money is it?"

"He wouldn't say."

We thought about it for a bit.

"Maybe it *is* true," she said.

"It's not true."

Still, the call kept tickling at me. The one thing that prevented me from dismissing it entirely was the fact that I actually didn't know much about my father's side of the family. After Dad died, we fell out of touch with them all, and even when he was alive, we rarely saw any of his relatives other than his sister, our aunt Jane.

Dad used to take us to Aunt Jane's to hang out with our cousins, two girls close to us in age. I liked visiting them, mostly because Aunt Jane kept her house well stocked with snacks. And not "snacks," like the healthy crap Mom tried to pass off on us, handfuls of baby carrots and tiny boxes of raisins and shit like that. Real snacks containing real American corn syrup. Fruit Roll-Ups and Cracker Jack and Doritos. The kinds of snacks any child would be proud to consume. My own house held no such wonders. "Have an apple" was my mother's favorite reply to our repeated complaints that we had nothing good to eat in the house, as if she didn't know that apples were precisely the kind of garbage we were complaining about. But other than enjoying their good snacks and the fact that my cousins were allowed to watch MTV in their basement playroom, I didn't feel one way or another about hanging out with them. They were just kind of around, an immutable fact of our upbringing.

I have no treasured memories from those days. Mostly, we spent our time together loitering on their local playground, or just trawling the neighborhood streets. It seems strange now to recall a time when children were allowed to wander unsupervised across the vast suburban landscape like refugees, but that's what we did. When Eric and I fell out of touch with them after Dad died, I didn't feel too much about it other than the occasional twinge of mild guilt at having given away something I knew to be valuable even if I couldn't exactly identify what. Mostly, though, I didn't think about them at all, because thinking about my aunt and cousins meant thinking about my dad, and even fifteen years after the fact, I still hadn't come to terms with his death.

(I am not going to write about his death here because I did so in my previous book. I also told the story on the radio show *This American Life*. If you are interested, I would suggest buying the book since I don't receive royalties from *This American Life* because the host, Ira Glass, is a son of a bitch.*)

As I thought some more about the call offering me a mysterious inheritance, an unsettling possibility began percolating in my mind. Perhaps the situation was the exact opposite of what I believed it to be. Perhaps a long-lost uncle hadn't suddenly popped into existence. Perhaps, instead, we were the ones who had disappeared. After all, an entire side of my family was still out there somewhere, but from their point of view, it was we who had vanished. It must have seemed to them as if we'd died along with Dad.

An envelope bearing the name of a fussy-sounding law firm arrived a few days later. Inside, I found an affidavit asking me to affirm that I was who I said I was. Which I did; I am me, so says I. The letter asked for no money, no personal information like my Social Security number. Just a straightforward-seeming legal document. These con artists were very, very good.

I called my brother. He'd received the same call, the same letter, harbored the same doubts. We discussed the likelihood of fraud. But as we talked, we began doubting our doubts.

"Maybe it's true," he said.

"Maybe it's true," I said.

---

* I am joking about Ira Glass. He is a lovely and generous man, and I am not just saying that in anticipation of asking him to blurb my book.

My father's father was a cop. He joined the NYPD in 1941, right before America entered WWII, but his police work in Harlem excused him from military service because, as my aunt says, "Our own war was pretty hot in Harlem." Grandpa Leon spent about thirty years in the force, eventually rising to assistant borough commander in Queens, an impressive rise for a first-generation Jewish-American cop. My memories of him are dim. While Dad was alive we didn't see Grandpa much; after Dad died, we never saw him again. The vague impression I have of him is of a large, taciturn man with a Walt Disney mustache and a Tony Soprano gut. I ask Jane what growing up with him was like. "Unhappy," she says. Her parents fought frequently, and Leon kept the household on edge.

"Was he a yeller?"

No, she told me, worse. When he and my grandmother fought, rather than yell and be done with it, he would shut down, sometimes for weeks at a time. He closed off the entire world: family members, friends, neighbors, everybody. A heavy, ugly silence filled the house like carbon monoxide, choking off all conversation. "It was like living with a dead man," she says.

"Nice," I think. "Very mature." A second later, though, I realize that I do the same thing. When Martha and I fight, she yells and I disengage. The more she screams, the more I curl up into myself, until she is left arguing with a hedgehog. Never for weeks, though. A few days at the most. Not because I want to nurse the grudge, but because once I burrow into my own head, it's tough for me to dig my way out again, and also because it sometimes takes a few days for her to even realize I am not speaking to her.

Given his introversion, perhaps it is not surprising that Grandpa didn't maintain close relationships with anyone, not his son or his son's kids, or his siblings. He had two—a sister, Ruth, and a brother, Seymour. Ruth and Seymour married a brother and sister whose last name was Pincus, which seems wrong somehow, but I guess is okay in the eyes of the law and the Lord.

Sometime in the '70s, Seymour and his wife, Pearl, moved to South Florida with their only son, Marc. Pearl died. Marc died. Ruth died. My grandfather died. Seymour was the only one left. When he finally died, he did so without a will, which meant his estate would pass to his nearest living relatives: Aunt Jane and Dad's children, the three of us. That's when I got a phone call at work from a man used to being called a liar. A few weeks later, I signed for an envelope from FedEx. Inside was another envelope. Inside that envelope was a check.

It was true.

In my hand, I held an envelope containing one-third of one-half of my dearly beloved uncle Seymour's estate. I didn't know how much money I was about to inherit, but I figured it had to be a lot. Why else would they go to all the trouble of tracking us down? The only times people track other people down is to collect a bounty or to give them fantastic sums of money. I figured, at a minimum, I was probably looking at a couple hundred thousand dollars. As for the maximum, well, I supposed the maximum could be anything. A million dollars. A billion dollars. Possibly even a zillion dollars. Regardless of the exact amount, it was clear my life was about to change forever.

I opened the envelope and looked at the check: $3,280.

My life was not about to change forever.

A little perspective: On any other occasion, I would be thrilled to receive, out of the blue, a check for three grand. That's a lot of money to get for answering the phone. But in these very specific, once-in-a-lifetime circumstances—mystery man on the other end of the phone, long-lost uncle, notarized documents, unspecified sum of money—it's hard to view three thousand dollars as anything other than a disappointment. It's like the universe tossed me a few Ben

Franklins and went, "Here, you greedy, covetous prick. Don't spend it all in one place." Well, guess what, universe? I *did* spend it all in one place. I bought a new laptop computer, a printer, and some books about poker. The only inheritance I am ever likely to receive squandered in a twenty-minute online shopping binge. Worse, the books I bought probably cost me another three grand in poker losses.

So that was the end of that, at least until a month or so later, when I received a letter from Aunt Jane, the first time I'd heard from her in years. She'd gotten my address from the law firm that handled the estate. Whatever guilt I'd felt about losing my relationship with her and my cousins, she confessed to feeling a hundredfold in her letter to me, which in turn, made *me* feel a hundred times worse on top of that.

Jane apologized for having lost contact with me and my siblings all those years ago. She filled me in on our cousins' lives, and hers. She lived (like everybody else in my family) in South Florida with a new husband and a menagerie of yippy little dogs. Life was good, she wrote, and she felt so happy to be back in touch. I wrote back, filling her in on my own life: wife, baby boy, global television super-star. We agreed to get together the next time I came down to Florida to visit Mom.

Sometimes when I wake up in the morning, I inadvertently ad-just my torso a certain way so that my hip lets out a sudden crack, bursting apart some long-held tension I hadn't even been aware I'd been carrying. That's what seeing Aunt Jane again felt like. When we finally met, maybe six months later, she wrapped me in a big hug and I felt some small, pained part of me slip back into place. That's what family is, I guess—finding a place for all the parts of ourselves that fit nowhere else.

We sat and talked, and her response to everything I said was "Wonderful, wonderful, wonderful" in the slight Queens accent she'd carried south with her. Chatting with my aunt felt like rediscovering some long-forgotten foreign language. It brought me right back to those summer afternoons in my cousins' basement sucking on ice pops while the grown-ups talked upstairs. I imagine it must have been weird for her, seeing me for the first time in decades, now grown with a family of my own, about the same age her brother was when he died.

I don't mean to exaggerate the evening. All we really did was eat dinner and chat and play with those yippy dogs. We talked about Dad. We toured her home. We did what people do. And when the evening ended, we hugged again and promised to stay in touch, which we have done, although more sporadically than I think either of us would like, but enough so that now and again we get together, and now and again, she answers my e-mail questions about what it was like to grow up unhappy with a cop who didn't talk.

I've since grown reacquainted with my cousins, too, and their husbands, and now their kids. Once a year, we all assemble for an afternoon to catch up on each other's lives. My brother burns hamburgers on the infrared grill he bought because he read somewhere that infrared is the best kind of grill (we share the same bad genes, so he, too, is a gullible idiot). As the afternoon is ending, we tie the children together with rope so we can take a group photo without them scattering in every direction. We hang out. It's a small thing, an afternoon with family. But it's my inheritance. And it's wonderful, wonderful, wonderful.

CHAPTER FIVE

I feel bad about my feet

My reconnection with Jane was one of my rare family inheritances that did not disappoint. Most of them—mystery money, spiritual agita, bad genes—wound up being more burden than windfall. But the one I feel worst about is my feet. I feel bad about my feet. They are unsightly things, flappy and textured like the bumpy sides of Ping-Pong paddles. They are the anatomical equivalent of deli meat that has been left out too long. They are, in a word, fetid.

Of all my foot problems, the worst and most obvious is onycho-mycosis, aka "ringworm of the nails." If there is a more horrid-sounding combination of words than "ringworm of the nails," I don't know what it is. The first thing you need to know about this condition is that ringworm isn't actually a worm. It is so named because physicians coined the term *ringworm* in the fifteenth century to describe the circular red rash they found on patients. They thought it looked kind of wormy, so they named it ringworm, the better to horrify all future generations.

The actual cause of ringworm is fungus. As a term, *fungal infection* is not much better than ringworm, calling to mind jungle rot, poisonous mushrooms, and the sorts of black mold that cause people to burn their own homes to the ground. Fungi are not evil by nature; like all living things, all they want is to survive. They do this by feasting on keratin, the stuff that makes toenails and hair and rhino horns. (No word on whether rhinos get "ringworm of the horn.") Fungi eat keratin with the same reckless abandon with which I consume Taco Bell. As such, once they took up residence on my feet, they ensured themselves a steady food source as long as my body continues making toenails, which it will for a long time because, in all modesty, I am a toenail-making stud. The result is that my nails are thick, yellowed, and caked with chalky white stuff that has the powdery consistency of Cheez-It dust.

Once I asked a doctor about medical treatments. He told me that such a treatment exists but suggested I not take it because the medication could damage my liver. Plus, he told me that many times the fungus (properly called *dermatophytes*) just returns, anyway. What about the topical stuff they sell? He shrugged and said it didn't work. What should I do? He suggested I live with it. So live with it is what I have done.

Eric was the first to contract it, which means my present condition is his fault, just as all my problems can ultimately be laid in the lap of another. This was during our early teenage years when we shared a bedroom, and somehow his fungi migrated to my toenails. The stuff is allegedly contagious, yet I have never spread it to my wife, despite the fact that I have had considerably closer physical contact with my wife than my brother.

Until that point, my body and I had basically been simpatico. Yes, I'd had chicken pox, which left a couple small indentations on my nose, but nothing I would have pointed to as a definitive physical flaw. The toenails changed that. Then came the zits. Then came the flab and thinning hair and all the rest. But the toenails were first, and as such, they deserve the honor of being the first body part about which I felt actual shame. The first time I worried about what other people would think should they see them, because I have never outgrown the playground fear of other children pointing at me and laughing.

Something as simple as woebegone toenails can actually have a profound effect on the way you conduct your life. I have spent many hours trying to conceal my feet from unprepared eyes. Every trip to the seashore is a carefully choreographed sequence of walking to the beach, removing my sneakers, burrowing my feet beneath the sand while shuffling toward the water, and then engaging in artful misdirection ("Look at all the seagulls!") as I arrange myself at our beaching spot before plunging my feet back under the sand for the duration of our stay, the way leaky nuclear reactors require entombment in concrete. Were unsuspecting beachgoers to see my feet, it would be like *Jaws* in reverse, hordes of people running into the water to escape. If an actual great white ever roams the shallows where I am sunbathing, it's a real question which fate the beachgoers would choose to suffer, my toenails or the shark.

During my single days, I conducted entire relationships without my partner once seeing my toenails. I did this with strategic lighting, cunning sheet dispersal, and the occasional besocked lovemaking. In fact, while shooting a love scene in a movie called *Wet Hot American Summer*, a movie about camp counselors, I suggested that my sex scene with *People* magazine's future Sexiest Man Alive Bradley Cooper be shot with the two of us wearing tube socks. Although I pitched the idea for its comedic effect, the real reason was to avoid anybody seeing my feet. Thankfully, the director agreed, or else the movie would have made even fewer dollars in the theaters than it actually did, which was already very close to zero dollars.

To her credit, Martha did not leave me upon first seeing my feet. Maybe she'd already resigned herself to moderate revulsion after seeing the rest of my unclothed body. Or maybe True Love can triumph over even toenail fungus. She has never once vomited when I removed my socks, and only several thousand times has she looked at my feet and asked, "Why don't you do something about that?"

She's right, of course. I really should take care of it. Any associated liver damage will pale in comparison to the joy I will surely experience strutting the world shorn of footwear. Grass upon my feet! Sand between my toes! The squish of warm animal turds underfoot! Even with a diseased liver, it would be a far better life than the one I am leading, a life of desperation and podiatric subterfuge.

So yes, I feel bad about my toenails, but the rest of my feet are not much better. The toes themselves each have a sprinkling of unsightly hair, and a mossy ruff of foot hair runs along the flat plane from my first and second toes to the foothills of my ankles. One may pluck toe hair, of course, as I sometimes do in the shower but, like locusts, it returns, in ever more virulent numbers. Why do feet need furry protection, anyway? We are not hobbits. Moreover, why do we even need toes? They seem so anachronistic, unsightly throwbacks to a time before the advent of cotton poly-blend socks and memory-foam sneakers. Sure, they help to keep us upright, but isn't there some more attractive solution to the vexing problem of bipedalism? We deserve better than these creepy, wriggling foot digits. We deserve modern, space-age toes, toes that glow in the dark and provide Wi-Fi connectivity. Maybe Apple can start designing toes.

As if my toe hair and nail fungus were not gross enough, the bottoms of my feet are also abhorrent. They have the same crumbly texture as the original draft of the Declaration of Independence. Cracked and peely, they are more snakeskin than human. I have no idea why the undersides of my feet should produce so much white and flaky derma. I already have dandruff on my head; why do I also need it on my feet? Sometimes I pick at the dead skin, drawing off long strips of people jerky, which I ball up between my fingers and flick to the floor like foot boogers. This activity only ends once I have accidentally peeled away some live skin, bloodying myself, and giving me painful foot lacerations that leave me limping for days.

God, I hate my feet.

I am not alone. Lots of people hate their feet. Feet are one of the most disliked body parts, along with legs and butts and noses. Even mostly naked *Sports Illustrated* swimsuit model Chrissy Teigen, possessed of a perfect body hand-forged from equal parts steel and Marshmallow Fluff, confessed to hating her own feet when I asked which is her least favorite body part. "Seriously," she said. "It's in my contracts that I will not show my feet."

I mention this to prove the point that even beautiful people hate their feet, but more importantly, to let you know that I am friends with a *Sports Illustrated* swimsuit model.

(On Twitter.)

(But still.)

Why do so many people hate their feet? My guess is it has something to do with their general lack of élan. Nobody has ever remarked, "Say, look at the classy set of feet on that dame!" They might give such a compliment to her legs or eyes or bazongas, but her feet? No. Even ballerinas, the classiest dames of all, bind their feet in thick reams of duct tape, yet still their feet end up as bloody messes. Feet are simply unbeautiful, their functions too utilitarian, the tasks they are called upon to perform too menial to garner much love.

(I am, of course, discounting the opinions of foot fetishists because fetishists, by nature, derive sexual satisfaction from those things, like feet and automotive tailpipes, that the rest of us do not.)

As I write these words, I am alone in my house, the kids in school, Martha at work. Our floors have radiant heating, and I ought to be enjoying their warmth barefoot, but I cannot bring myself to do so. Even when there is no danger of anybody besides me seeing them, I still cannot bear to keep my feet unclothed. What if I should happen to look down and see my toes, the ten of them splayed upon the ground like so many defrosted fish sticks? No, my feet must stay locked away, the way families used to hide crazy relatives in the attic.

When the kids were younger, I used to play "This Little Piggy" with them, that rhyming game when you go toe by toe explaining what each "piggy" was doing: going to the market, eating roast beef, being denied roast beef, etc. Both of my kids had perfect little feet: pink, soft, and squidgy. I used to like playing that silly game with them just before bed, especially the last part when the final little toe goes crying, "Wee, wee, wee all the way home," accompanied by tickles that ran up their legs and onto their bellies. One night when she was maybe three or four, my daughter said she wanted to do the piggy game on me. With some reluctance, I took off my socks. She stared at my thick, yellowy toenails for a second and asked me what was the matter with them. I told her my toenails were sick. "Okay," she said and proceeded to grab them, one by one, counting off all the little piggy activities until she got to the last one, and we laughed as she tickled me wee, wee, wee, all the way home. When we finished laughing, I told her she had better go wash her hands.

People love hands. We put diamonds on them. Not so with feet. The best jewelry feet get are three-dollar toe rings that turn green in the shower. Feet are the hand's trailer park cousins. Where hands are held and celebrated and soaked in rosewater, feet are ignored and stubbed against bed corners and scrubbed with rough pumice stones. Even I, hater of feet, believe they deserve better, squat monsters though they be. Feet are the body's blue-collar guys, the ones keeping us upright when we haul our fat asses off bar stools at the end of the night. They should write country songs about feet. But they don't, because even guitar-strumming cowboys who love everything American hate American feet. That's why they cover them with cowboy boots. The only Americans who *don't* cover their feet are hippies, and the only thing people hate more than feet is hippies.

CHAPTER SIX

Sponsored by Yoplait

Little by little, Mom's body started falling apart. Although she had a brief respite of good health after her scare with the tumor, within weeks she found herself back at the doctor's office with a couple of internal hernias.

Hernias don't seem like a big deal because most of the time they're not, although they sound downright harrowing when you find out what they actually are. A typical hernia occurs when the intestines poke their way through a hole in the abdominal wall. I once had a hernia of my own, a golf-ball-size lump that popped out of my groin one day like a particularly upsetting jack-in-the-box. When I pushed on it, I was actually pushing on my own intestines, as if I were an extra in the opening minutes of *Saving Private Ryan.*

My mom's hernias were of a different and more dangerous variety. An internal hernia occurs when some organ, usually the bowels, loops itself through a hole in a tissue wall. The protrusion created from this goes inward instead of outward, hence the "internal" designation. It's an uncommon condition, generally the result of severe trauma. Left untreated, an internal intestinal hernia can kill you. So why was my mom experiencing an ailment that more commonly occurs after a gunshot wound?

When she asked, her doctor said, "Like we told you, the internal radiation we gave you could destroy your insides."

The treatment for her cancer could *destroy* her insides?

Mom did not recall her medical team telling her any such thing but, then again, she is the same woman who doesn't remember what God Almighty told her either, so who knows if they warned her or not? Not that it would have mattered, she says, because even knowing the risks, she wouldn't have refused the radiation, explaining to me, "What was I going to do? Say I don't want to take the chance of having a couple internal hernias—I'll just die?"

Upon cutting her open to treat the hernias, they discovered, as predicted, that her insides had been "eaten away." Tissue had been damaged, turning her guts into vichyssoise. Not good. Nor did her medical team provide much reason for optimism. They told her that her condition would continue to get "worse and worse and worse."

That year, Mom begged us all to come down to Florida for Thanksgiving, believing it would be her last. I love my mother and I love Thanksgiving, but I hate Florida so much that even under the circumstances, going there seemed like a lot to ask.

But, of course, we went. What's left of my mother's family dutifully assembled in her pop-up community: Martha and I, my brother and his wife, our sister Susan, Mom's brother and his son, along with Sandy's parents, daughters, and their respective spouses. We gathered to celebrate the holiday, to be with my mom, and to savor the fragility of life. The food was terrible.

For all the sons out there who fetishize their mother's recipes for meatballs or matzo ball soup or macaroni, let me express my envy. When I was growing up, my mother's best dish was store-bought Entenmann's chocolate chip cookies. She speaks now as if she used to spend all her time in the kitchen preparing healthful, delicious menus. The truth, however, is that for most of my childhood, our dinners were a rotating selection of three dishes: linguini with canned clam sauce, cold tuna salad mixed with elbow macaroni, and broiled chicken served with peas. Anything else we consumed required microwaving. Mom and her previous partner Elaine kept our freezer stocked with frozen fish, frozen chicken nuggets, frozen pizza, frozen French toast, frozen Tater Tots, and frozen shaved-beef sandwiches known by the optimistic brand name Steak Tonight. By the time our family assembled in Florida for what we believed could be Mom's last Thanksgiving, she had given up any pretense of cooking whatsoever. Dinner was uninspired takeout served on paper plates and eaten with plastic utensils. Sure, Mom may have believed herself to be dying, but c'mon, lady, mash some damned potatoes.

Mom and Sandy's relationship was new enough that I still felt awkward around them, and especially around Sandy's children, neither of whom I knew, both of whom were also newly wed. All these new families coming together. The entire weekend felt like a trying-too-hard movie on the Hallmark Channel. It had everything: the lesbian couple, their various children with their various interfaith and/or interracial partners (Sandy's daughter's husband was African American), and even the spunky Down syndrome daughter, all celebrating the life of the matriarch in her final performance, sponsored by Yoplait.

The worst part about the weekend occurred when Mom took Eric and me aside for a private, teary soliloquy about how much she loved us. It was one of those squirmy talks Mom has occasionally subjected us to throughout our lives when she's feeling sentimental. Not yet having children myself, I couldn't comprehend her strange desire to pour her love on us all at once, the way football players dump Gatorade on their coaches. Why she couldn't just leave well enough alone? Why did she have to *say* things?

Now that I am a father, though, I know exactly what she was

trying to do; she wanted to convey the full depth and breadth of her love for us in case something tragic should happen before we met again. It was an impossible task. There's no way to compress the enormity of a parent's love for her children into a strained and mawkish five-minute conversation in a Florida town house; besides, I don't think anything of merit has *ever* been said in the suburbs of Fort Lauderdale. And for all of her fumbling effort, she needn't have bothered—we already knew.

Whatever failings she believes herself to have, Mom has always told us she loves us. We heard it every day growing up. She hugged us and reached into the backseat of the car while driving to give our legs painful love squeezes. She could yell, too, with the best of them, but even while facing her fury over failing grades or unmade beds, I never felt unloved. I took being loved for granted, and I think any success I have in my life is at least partly attributable to that simple statement.

Some people worry about becoming their parents when they become parents themselves, but I took a couple of Mom's parenting lessons to heart. For one thing, I try to make my kids read every night before bed. I don't care what they read, but they are supposed to spend at least half an hour before bed reading *something*. Also, I make them run errands with me on occasion, taking one kid or the other, even though I know they will be bored waiting on line with me to buy stamps or roaming the aisles of the supermarket. Mom did this with us, and now I know why: Spending time together one-on-one is good. Plus, they're usually able to wheedle some piece-of-garbage snack out of me as payment for their time. But the most important thing I do is tell my kids I love them. I tell them every day, several times a day.

"I love you," I say to Elijah as he leaves for school every morning, and when I close the door to his room at night. His response, if he responds at all, toggles between "Yeah" and "I know." My daughter Ruthie is still young enough to respond with an enthusiastic "Love you, too!" but I know already the day is fast approaching when she will withdraw from my affections just as Elijah already has, as I withdrew from Mom's when I was his age, not because I loved her any less, but because loving my mom felt so uncool. Regardless, I know they hear me. I know because I heard Mom all those years, even when I was ignoring her, even when I was giving her the metaphorical and literal finger; after all, telling a parent to fuck off is one of the great joys of adolescence. I did it a lot.

But there was no fuckoffery to be had that Thanksgiving Day in Florida. Eric and I forced ourselves to endure her affections, the way Elijah now suffers my good-night forehead kisses. Mom wanted to know if we are happy. Yes, we assured her, we're happy. She wanted us to know that we're good people. Yes, we assured her, we know we're good people. But most importantly, she wanted us to know that I had always been her favorite.

Although Mom believed herself to be in her final days, I could see no indication that this was the case. It was a deathbed conversation without the deathbed. Yes, her health was bad and her long-term prognosis worse, but I saw no signs of the Reaper hovering about. No scythe marks on the floor. No rattling chains. She seemed, if not well, then at least okay. Or maybe I was just in denial, which in addition to being a sound medical strategy, is also the best way to cope with emotions.

My instinct is to pull away from difficult situations, to detach, make jokes. I tried being present for Mom during our talk, but it was hard. I felt like she was trying to create something momentous for us from dubious materials, the way Richard Dreyfuss builds Devils Tower out of mashed potatoes in *Close Encounters of the Third Kind*. The whole time I was thinking, "Okay, wrap it up." But even though our conversation felt awkward as hell, and even though she didn't say anything we hadn't heard a thousand times before, I love her for trying.

I left Florida a couple days later, inexplicably guilt-ridden. Why did I feel so bad? I'd done my part. I'd suffered through the dry turkey and wet conversation. I'd made the appropriate amount of small talk with Sandy's kids and their husbands. I'd been a good guest and son. But I left feeling as if I had let Mom down, maybe because I felt like Mom was asking me for something I couldn't give, some words I didn't know how to speak about love and acceptance and forgiveness.

A parent never has the right words to describe their love for a child. There's only a dull ache where words should be. If it were a sound, a parent's love would sound like this: "Mmmmphhhf." So when a parent tries to express that love in its fullest form to their kids, it comes out wrong. The best any parent can do is just to be there, time after time after time, when they need you and when they don't, and when they do but don't know it. You show up and, in showing up, you hope they get the message.

When I lie dying, sometime in the distant future, I am going to do the opposite of what Mom did to Eric and me. Instead of saddling them with heavy expressions of love, I will summon my children to my deathbed, make them lean in close, then whisper, "You're both a couple of assholes." And if they laugh, I'll know I did my job.

CHAPTER SEVEN

We are those assholes now

Home for me, as I said, is the wilds of Connecticut. Martha and I have been here twelve years and plan on staying. Like most of our neighbors, we are transplants, crowded out of nearby New York City by congestion and high rents and the sound of Japanese superbikes bombing past our window at three in the morning. We moved here to slow down, to trade New York City's roaches and rats for moths and mice, to have space to breathe, elbow room in which to flex our elbows, safe outdoor spaces for the children to complain about being forced to play upon. And of course we moved here for the schools. Everybody wants to know about the schools.

"AREN'T THE SCHOOLS GREAT?!" our friends and neighbors yell at each other over bottomless, frothy cups of no-fat decaf soy lattes, which is another way of asking, "Aren't WE great?!" We ask because we need somebody—anybody—to affirm our life choices. We did the right thing, didn't we? We're doing what's best for our children, aren't we? We are smart and worthwhile and our work lives are fulfilling and our spiritual lives are rich and our communities are litter-free and we are going to live forever. Right?

These are the sorts of questions we ask ourselves while lying

awake at night listening to our hearts chattering in our chests. As
we breathe the country air, tart and sweet as a slice of cheddar on
fresh-baked apple pie. As we enjoy the restful night music of coyotes
ripping apart baby deer. As we feel the Lyme disease clawing its way
into our nervous systems. We take Ambien to turn off our heads,
but it doesn't work. Maybe that chattering in our chests isn't anxiety
but the first spastic stutter step of atrial fibrillation. Maybe we won't
wake up in the morning. We are slowly going crazy. I don't know if
it's all the unnerving silence or what, but put enough soft city folks
into the deep and shadowy woods together and they are bound to
freak the fuck out. It's like *Lord of the Flies* up here, wardrobe by
J.Crew.

Our occupations and circumstances vary, but we share certain
commonalities. We are well educated and well-off and mostly white.
We made good life choices. We drive good, safe cars. On Sunday
nights in the warm weather, we gather on the public lawn with pic-
nic dinners of roasted veggies and baked chicken and listen to free
concerts while the kids play tag out by the gazebo. We share a peculiar state of mind whereby we have everything but cannot stop
complaining about it. It's not that we are dissatisfied, exactly; more
that we know something better is just around the bend. We want to
do better, be better, feel better, *be* better.

We control what we can but so little feels within our control. Our
kids are all growing up too fast. Soon they'll be gone. Soon we'll be
alone in these houses that used to suffer their handprints on every
stainless-steel surface, crumbs lodged in every crevice, unidentifi-
able stains smearing every wall. They will be gone but our houses
will be clean and we will be despondent. We can't keep our kids
from growing up and we can't keep ourselves from growing old. But
we try. We attend daily services at SoulCycle and spend our Sun-
days worshipping at the church of Whole Foods. No, we cannot
beat back time, but we can smooth our skin and tone our abs and

visit hair-restoration specialists in the city. We can armor ourselves against the future with pearlescent teeth and manicured nails and buns of steel.

But the woods are dark and they are closing in.

Just because I recognize our insanity does not immunize me from it. Far from it. If anything, I am among the worst of my kind, vain and fearful, scrambling to figure out how to keep myself alive. Today and tomorrow and always. And if I cannot do that due to my bad, bad genes, then I will settle for keeping myself attractive. Starting with my waist.

Only a few years ago, my pant measurement was a snappy 30/32. That's a waist-and-inseam combo any man would be proud to call his own. 30/32. You can almost hum it. But now, suddenly—alarmingly—the numbers are equal: 32/32. No longer quite so zippy. Said aloud, it's an alarming jangle of syllables, as untrustworthy as people whose first and last names are the same: Steve Stevens. I wouldn't buy even buy a paper clip from a guy named Steve Stevens.

If I allow this trend to continue, very soon my waist measurement will exceed my inseam measurement. What then? What happens when I am wider around than I am tall as measured from crotch to ankle? Surely that is the beginning of the end, as prophesized in the book of Atkins. As a younger man, I swore I would never let such a thing occur; you can easily make such promises to yourself when you are twenty-five and the weight does not accrue no matter how many Taco Bell #3 Value Meals you consume.

For the first forty years of my life, any weight gained was good weight, weight that would fill me out, broaden my shoulders, add girth to my loins. But now it appears I am past my metabolic prime and have entered the long, slow glide path into general flabbiness, soon to be followed by bloat, diabetes, leaky, corrugated arteries, and, eventually, a final descent into a morbid obesity so profound a crane will be required to extract me from my bedroom window, where I will one day be discovered in my bed, wrapped in a sheet, lying facedown in a viscous pool of coagulated KFC chicken gravy.

These are the kinds of thoughts that keep me staring at the ceiling during the wee morning hours. But I take comfort in the woolly optimism of my woodsy brethren and sisters. We hearty pioneers of the Connecticut wilderness are nothing if not resilient. Where anxiety might paralyze those in lesser zip codes, here we let it motivate us, activate us, inspire us. For we are the strivers and doers. We bear college degrees from good, private, second-tier schools. Our Internet connections are hearty, our search queries strong, and we do something about it.

The women inject themselves into constrictive Lycra suits and do Pilates. The men squeeze their testicles into compression shorts and go for long, winding rides on artisanal bicycles hand-carved from asteroids. Both sexes take to witchcraft, reciting impenetrable incantations: *antioxidant, beta-carotene, Botox, ohm. . . .* We offer burnt sage to Gwyneth, goddess of Dewy Skin.

Where once Martha and I talked about rock bands and theater and other urban pleasures, we now have regular conversations about fiber. We stock up on olives because it is understood that olives are healthful and delicious. Turmeric, that wonderful Indian spice, is healthful and delicious. Red meat is healthful and delicious every ten days but eaten more than that renders it heart-killing and carcinogenic. Kale is magic. Beets: holy. Once a week or so, we dutifully consume some bland species of (sustainable) (wild, not farm-raised) fish. We even go so far as to add flaxseed to recipes that do not call for flaxseed because we are those assholes now.

Assholes yes, but not saints. We still let our kids eat crap. Not exclusively, but enough that they do not feel as though they are growing up on an Israeli kibbutz or, worse, in Park Slope, Brooklyn. And when we buy that crap for them to eat, of course, it means Martha and I eat it, too. The kale wilts in the produce drawer. The beets bleed out onto paper towels, unloved and untouched. And when I say we eat fish once a week, I am lying. It is more like once a month. It just feels like more often because having fish for dinner, even the sustainable kind, sucks.

Occasionally we try sneaking healthfulness into places where none ought to exist. One night I made mashed potatoes. Except there were no actual potatoes in my mashed potatoes. Instead, I used cannellini beans and parsnips pureed with chicken stock and roasted garlic, a recipe I found in one of those cookbooks that teach you how to eat so you will live to be a million.

"Why do the mashed potatoes look like that?" asked Elijah. It is true the dish had a peculiar tint that betrayed itself as something other than spud-like.

"I don't know what you're talking about," I replied. "Those are regular mashed potatoes."

"Okay," he said, accepting me at my word because he does not yet know his father is a liar and a fink.

Ruthie, although two and a half years younger, has a more finely attuned bullshit detector. She refused to even try the dish until threatened with expulsion from the dinner table. When she finally inserted a quavering forkful into her mouth, she moved the "mashed potatoes" around her tongue for a moment, choked back a vomit bubble, and pronounced them disgusting.

"They are not!" I replied. "They're delicious." She was right. They were disgusting.

Martha insisted she loved the dish, even eating Ruthie's unwanted portion. Then she complained that I "let her" eat too much. I let her? What would she have me do? Put a hand on her wrist as she lifted another forkful into her gob and say, "Sweetheart, I think you've had enough"? How would that have gone over? I suspect not very well.

Martha hates her body, or at least claims to, despite the fact that she looks great. I'm not just saying that as a husband whose wife will one day read this book. I speak as a fan and connoisseur of the female form, as evidenced by my regular habit of studying examples of it online after she goes to bed each night. But like everybody else's, Martha's relationship with her own body is fraught. "I look terrible," she says occasionally (every day).

Other regular complaints:

"I look old."

"I look fat."

"My hair is a disaster."

"Look at this!" she often yells at me. "This" usually means her stomach, which sometimes protrudes after a big meal, the inevitable result of once providing temporary housing for two freeloading fetuses. "This" might also mean a new spider vein on her leg or a twitchy eye muscle. I am forever being instructed to look at some misbehaving part of her anatomy.

I dislike when she does this, because I have no interest in finding fault with her. Not because I find her flawless, but because I am too susceptible to suggestion. If she keeps enumerating her failings, perhaps I will start believing her to be as monstrous as she believes herself to be, and I have no wish to think ill of her body. I love it too much. Plus, it would require too much negative mental energy, energy that could better be spent hating myself.

Personally, I am not a fan of bodies at all. They are too time-intensive, require too much maintenance. They must be tended to on an almost constant basis; if they don't need food, they need water. Or air. Brushing *and* flossing? Please. Bodies are nuisances. They are fragile. They suffer pain. They runneth over with fluids. Bodies demand recharging, not once in a while, but every single night. Moreover, they are prone to disruption and disrepair. Every body inevitably fails, as my mother's is slowly doing fifteen hundred miles to the south. They are the very definition of planned obsolescence. Bodies are simply not designed for today's go-go lifestyle. But what to do about it? How do we wring more usefulness out of these tetchy flesh bags?

There is a doctor in Italy who claims he can transplant human heads. His method for doing so is a disarmingly simple three-step process:

1. Sever the spinal cords of both head and body donors.
2. Fit them together like store mannequins.
3. Stick the two together with "inorganic polymer glue."

It sounds like the sort of plan a six-year-old might devise. Yet, as improbable as the idea sounds, it might actually be possible. Similar experiments have already been conducted on both dogs and monkeys with varying levels of success. In the first half of the twentieth century, Soviet scientists attempted to keep disembodied dogs alive by hooking their heads up to a device called an "autojector," which was a big fluid recycling system, sort of like a swimming pool pump. How successful these experiments were is a matter of some debate, although footage exists on YouTube of a rather sad-looking Siberian husky head being coaxed to eat a piece of cheese. The "dog" eats the cheese, which then falls out the bottom of its neck. The footage is possibly a hoax, but whether it is or isn't, please don't watch, because seeing a bodiless dog head trying to eat cheese is a genuine bummer.

In 1970, an American scientist named Robert White transplanted the head of one rhesus monkey onto the body of another. Although the monkey (monkeys?) survived the procedure, the poor creature could not do much more than look around, because the operation destroyed its spinal column.

Forty-five years later, both glue and head-severing technology have apparently advanced so much that the aforementioned Dr.

Frankenstini argues that it is now possible for humans to regain at least some motor control after undergoing a head transplant. Think about that. Same head, different body. Or, from the point of view of the cadaver, same body, different head.

In fact, as of this writing, it has been announced that the first head transplant will be attempted sometime within the next few years. A Russian man, suffering from a terminal muscle-wasting disease, has volunteered to be the first patient. The operation, at an anticipated cost of fifteen million dollars, will be performed in China, a country that has fewer restrictions on doing insane shit.

Imagine: the ability to cast off our old, wrinkled carcasses with their unsightly waist/inseam sizes in exchange for new, toned, tight bodies with clear, unsullied toenails. From there it's conceivable that, in the next few decades, we'll have the ability to grow headless bodies on big industrial body farms, swapping them out as easily as we snap on and off vacuum attachments.

At that point, everybody could have a "perfect body," or a custom-made imperfect one. Or a body with nine legs. Or maybe we could transplant our torsos onto horse bodies and become centaurs. And, of course, once we are centaurs, we are only one step away from becoming flying centaurs, and then it's basically game over because there's nothing more awesome than that.

But until that day arrives, we are stuck with the bodies we have. You with yours, me with mine. Everybody deals with their bodies in different ways. Some people do everything they can to maximize their body's powers and abilities. Many more people, people such as myself, *think* about maximizing their body's powers and abilities, but mostly eat Tostitos and stale almond cookies with dog hairs pressed into them. Working out is hard and upsetting. Eating well is hard and upsetting. Sitting around doing nothing is easy and anesthetizing, which is why I prefer it.

But "easy and anesthetizing" is not a good long-term survival

strategy. If I am going to live long enough to become a flying cen-
taur, I need to do something beyond adding flaxseed to my oatmeal.
Which brings me back to the cult of well-being here in the woods
of Connecticut. Yes, one could find fault with our healthful obses-
sions, the way we careen from fad diet to fad exercise regimen to
fad supplement like a crew of lost sailors trying to navigate their
way through the fog. But you cannot fault our enthusiasm for trying.
Here, people do not wait for things to go from bad to worse. They
don't even wait for them to get bad. They wear Fitbits to track their
physical exertions and construct elaborate Excel spreadsheets docu-
menting each calorie that enters their mouths. They have action
plans. I wanted an action plan, too.

I resolved to change my ways. Preserving a respectable pant
measurement provided some motivation. Seeing Mom ailing and
bedbound provided more. She would give anything to have my mobility, so what was I doing sitting around letting my own good health
escape like air from a leaky bicycle tire? I couldn't rely on science to
save me, or faith, or even denial. I needed to activate some dormant
part of my brain, the part that notices a beautiful day and thinks,
"Hey, I should be outside!" and not, "Hey, I think we still have a
bag of pretzels in the cupboard!" But I didn't know how to make the
change. It wasn't like I hadn't tried before. I had. And failed. Why
does doing difficult things have to be so damned difficult?

CHAPTER EIGHT

I do not know why my fantasy self so closely resembles a Hitler Youth leader

People who know me probably assume I have always been sedentary because I wear my laziness like a pair of bespoke footy pajamas. But I am actually a person of above-average hand-eye coordination, fleet of foot, handy with a rack of Scrabble tiles. I am good at catching any manner of spheroid object thrown in my direction. When pressed, I can swing a softball bat with moderate aptitude. And while it is true that I possess the upper-body strength of an anemic tween, my calves are naturally toned, and I can still give my daughter regular piggyback rides with only minimal back pain. In short, I am woeful but not yet wretched.

My body mass still hovers in the "normal" range, but I know better. That new glob of goop hugging my middle—the one that has, in recent years, occasionally caused me to utter those awful words "Can you let it out a little" to various costume designers working on various television shows—is a harbinger of fat to come, the first questionable resident in what used to be a decent neighborhood. I have a photograph of myself from when I was about twenty-three. My shirt is unbuttoned and, if I look closely, I can make out abs. Lots of them, stacked atop each other like croquet balls. But now those abs are hidden away, hibernating in a pillow fort constructed from pizza and buffalo wings.

Even when I was twenty-three, though, I felt distraught over my physical appearance: unhappy that I was too thin but simultaneously terrified to gain any weight. It's distressing to never feel good about how you look or to view your own appearance in graduated shades of "not bad." Which is weird, because I know myself to be a not-unattractive person. In fact, aside from all of my hideous deformities, I believe myself to be a fine-looking young man.

(Although I have already established that, from an actuarial standpoint, I am no longer young and am not even technically middle-aged, for the purposes of my already delicate self-image, it is important that I maintain the fiction of remaining a "young man.")

What's odd, though, is that the person I believe myself to be does not resemble the actual me at all. I don't just mean age. I mean, the person I see in my head when I think "me" doesn't much look like the me I see when I glance at a mirror. Does everybody have some other person who resides in their brain, some fantasy avatar? Well, I do. He is six feet tall, rangy, and lantern-jawed. His hair is the color of sand after a rainstorm. Basically, he looks like a Winklevoss twin. But his last name cannot be Winklevoss because that sounds like the name of one of Tinker Bell's friends. Besides, I am not so deranged that I would actually give my idealized vision of myself a name. But if I did, it would be Bruce Whitehall.

I do not know why my fantasy self so closely resembles a Hitler Youth leader.

Regardless, Bruce Whitehall has a swimmer's body: long, lean, broad at the shoulders, narrow at the waist. It is the kind of body I could perhaps achieve through hundreds of hours spent swimming laps in a pool, a task complicated only by the fact that I hate swimming. Swimming is horrible. It's the only activity I can think of that is exhausting, boring, and life-threatening all at the same time.

There is an excellent reason our species evolved *from* the water, not *toward* it. The reason is that it sucks being in any body of water that is not ninety-five degrees, bubbling, and in a boutique spa. Water is meant to be drunk, splashed upon bikini models like my best friend Chrissy Teigen, and frolicked in for no more than seven minutes at a time. The thought of voluntarily dredging one's body through endless laps in a chlorinated swimming pool is horrifying.

When I was a child, Mom forced Eric and me to take lessons at the local YMCA. These lessons followed the standard Red Cross program, which ranks swimming ability according to a system of ever more deadly fish, from "guppy" all the way up to "laser shark." Although I did eventually learn to survive in the water, I don't think I ever progressed much beyond "anchovy." My primary memories from those sessions are of cold water and cold changing rooms. All told, I probably got far more exercise from shivering than from swimming.

My own children seem much more at ease in the water. We gave them swim lessons, too, when they were younger, applying the same logic that Mom assuredly applied to us: Teaching your children how to survive in water is the best way of ensuring that you don't have to pay attention to them when they are near water. I know from first-hand experience how important this can be.

One of the most terrifying moments of my life occurred at a neighbor's pool party. There were probably fifty or sixty people there, most of them in the water or on the pool deck. Lots of kids. Too many kids to keep track of, really. Ruthie was about two at the time, playing at the edge of the pool by herself. I sat ten or fifteen yards away, my eyes sort of on her and sort of checking out how the local ladies looked in swimwear. As I dawdled on the pool deck sipping a beverage and ogling the neighbors, I happened to glance toward my daughter just as she toppled into the water. One moment she was watching the wake her pointer finger made as she dragged it through the water, the next she was fully underwater with barely a splash as evidence that she had ever been there at all. I sat far enough away to see that nobody else even noticed her go in. Thank goodness I have crippling social anxiety or I might have been talking to somebody instead of watching my daughter. I jumped in (shirt on because I feel bad about my chest) and hauled her, sobbing and choking, from the water. Total elapsed time: less than five seconds. Am I a hero? Sure, but that's not the point. The point is that children are stupid and parents need to give them every opportunity to survive their own stupidity.

So, off and on for about two years, we drove our kids to the local pool every Saturday morning for the same Red Cross lessons I endured as a child. I watched them progress from dunking their faces in the water, to jumping in without crying, to performing credible freestyle strokes, to glissading along the length of the pool. When the lessons ended, the kids were competent, happy laser sharks. My son, in particular, is a good swimmer, which I admire, although that admiration will turn quickly to seething resentment should he emerge from puberty with a Bruce Whitehall–esque build.

I knew that if I wanted to get into shape, swimming was not the answer for me. All exercise books recommend that anybody looking to improve their physical fitness should find an exercise or sport they enjoy. Never answered is the question, "What if you don't enjoy *any* exercise or sport?"

In my case, I could think of no physical activity that I was excited about enough to perform on a regular basis, which makes sense, because if such an activity existed I would already be doing it. I do enjoy playing poker but no matter how hard I tried, I could not quite convince myself that sitting, unmoving, at a card table for untold hours at a time counted as a sport.

Across the street from my house is a park boasting endless miles of mountain biking trails, apparently the best in the state. On weekends, scores of fit-looking dads unpack big-wheeled mountain bikes from the rumps of Subarus and disappear into those woods, emerging, hours later, mud-splattered and happy. With a little squinting, I could almost see myself pedaling through rushing streams, leaping atop fallen logs, surmounting boulders large and small, my helmet rakishly askew, perhaps an ascot poking from my yellow bicycling jersey, as I careen down sheer vertical slabs of granite.

"Maybe that's my sport," I thought. For what are naturally toned calves good for if not to put on display in biking shorts? "Yes," I thought. "Mountain biking is the sport for me." Mountain biking appealed to me in an "adventurous but not *too* adventurous" kind of way. Only the barest smidgen of self-awareness prevented me from rushing out and spending every dollar I had on one of those artisanal asteroid bikes. No, I would be prudent. Before committing to an expensive purchase, best to wait until I'd fully mastered the sport in a week or so.

Fortunately, my friend Matt had a mountain bike he wasn't using. Matt agreed to let me borrow the bicycle on a long-term basis, and I hauled the thing from New York City to Connecticut, got it tuned up at the local bike shop, bought myself a pair of padded bicycle shorts (which had the additional benefit of nicely flattering my cock), and pedaled for the woods. What I quickly realized upon encountering my first streams, fallen logs, and boulders, though, was that I had no idea what I was doing. The difference between riding a regular bicycle and riding this super-high-tech mountain bike amounted to the difference between flying a paper airplane and a jumbo jet, the main problem being that I had no idea what I was supposed to do with all the goddamned gears. There must have been a hundred of them. Maybe a thousand. Changing gears required manipulating a puzzling assortment of levers, and it seemed like every time I tried to go from a higher gear into a lower gear—or maybe it was vice versa—the goddamned chain would fall off the bike, necessitating a dismount to thread the goddamned thing back into the goddamned doohickey from which it fell. And when the chain wasn't falling off the bike, I was.

Then, while trying to leap over a giant (tiny) boulder (rock), I pitched myself forward over the handlebars and onto my ass. I am told this sort of thing happens all the time to mountain bikers. People fall down. They sprain joints. They break collarbones. What had I been thinking? Mountain biking was a dangerous and foolhardy sport, better left to guys named Austin or Sky or Cody, but Bruce Whitehall would not be mountain biking. I wheeled the bike into my garage, where it served as spiderweb scaffolding until Matt retrieved it a year later. Needless to say, I did not purchase my own mountain bike, although I do still sometimes wear my bike shorts around the house. They do not impress my wife.

Ultimately, wasn't impressing my wife and, by extension, the entire female population, the point of the endeavor? Yes, getting in shape provides health benefits and extends life span and blah dee blah dee blah. But if I'm being honest with myself, don't I really just want women to find me attractive? And no, I obviously don't mean *all* women. Just most. Say, seventy-five percent. After all, I am a married man.

Aren't my fears about growing old and getting fat and going bald and all the rest of it just symptoms of anxiety related to feeling unworthy of love? The reason Bruce Whitehall looks like Bruce Whitehall isn't that I particularly want to look like a Hitler Youth leader but that, in my mind, that's the kind of guy women find attractive (minus the Nazi part). And of course that's nonsense, but I can't shake the feeling that whatever my type happens to be is the wrong type. Moreover, why do I even care? I have a wife who loves me. Why do I need other (most) women to desire me? Only because I'm scared they don't. The need for female companionship and affection has been at my center for as long as I can remember, my self-esteem rising and falling on tides of estrogen. And while I know it is neither necessary nor healthy to seek validation from others, I can't help it. How much of our self-worth is tied up in the opinions of others? Yes, we all like to imagine ourselves as iconoclasts, hacking new trails across the tattered landscape of conventional thought. But that's a lie. For as much as we like to think that we are freethinkers who care not a whit what others think of us, I've never met anybody for whom that is true. Maybe the guy who hiked to Alaska in that book *Into the Wild,* but he wound up starving to death.

As for me, I cannot help but seek my own sustenance, at least in part, from Martha. I am at my happiest when I feel like she loves me, and my lowest when I feel she does not. It's always been that way with me and girls. Maybe this comes from being raised in a lesbian household. Or maybe I'm just codependent. It's not that I'm constantly seeking her approval in all things, but I do it often enough to recognize that I place nearly as much value on her opinions as I do on my own. When her favor does not come, I suffer from its absence. My desire to get into shape had as much to do with pleasing Martha as myself, even though Martha has once never told me she would prefer that I look a little bit more like a Hitler Youth leader. Then again, now that I think about it, it would have been odd if she had.

CHAPTER NINE

You down with ECT?

As awkward as our "You know I love you, right? RIGHT?!?" Thanksgiving conversation was, Mom and I have had worse. The most cringe-inducing occurred during my early teen years, when Mom and Elaine summoned me to the living room for a chat. That alone should have set off alarm bells, since the living room was sacrosanct. Even though our crummy town house barely accommodated the six human beings who lived there, the living room remained off-limits, the invisible threshold between foyer and living room as inviolable as a crime scene. Even our neglected English springer spaniel Winston knew enough not to go in there and he was a genuine idiot. Mom and Elaine reserved the living room for "entertaining," despite the fact they had few friends and almost never invited anybody over. The one exception I can remember was on the occasion of my mother's fortieth birthday, which, confusingly for a lesbian couple, involved a birthday cake shaped and decorated like a penis. The cake was delicious but, to this day, I have mixed emotions about enjoying it as much as I did.

On the rare occasions when I found myself the house's sole occupant, I would sometimes sneak into the living room to liberate candies from a neglected box of After Eight dinner mints kept secreted in a side table, and to peruse the pages of a coffee table book of "artistic photography," also kept hidden from prying adolescent eyes, which held more than a few (tastefully executed) shots of boobs. The forbidden living room, home to my every wanton desire. To be granted access to this sanctum foretold either very good tidings or very bad. Or, as it turned out, very weird.

After asking me to take a seat on the floor (just receiving an invitation to the living room did not include a guarantee of a seat on the actual furniture), Mom and Elaine gently explained to me that being gay was perfectly natural and normal, and certainly nothing to be ashamed of. I nodded. Right, right. Natural and normal, sure. No problem. But their lecture confused me. Why was I receiving this talk now, years after they'd gotten together? Had I said or done something to make them think I disapproved of their relationship? It's true that I did, but it had nothing to do with their homosexuality and everything to do with the fact that Elaine was a verbally abusive rage addict. Their homosexuality barely registered with me, no more noticeable to my eyes than their hairstyles. What insensitive remark had I made to merit this talking-to? I couldn't think of any. And then I realized: They weren't defending or justifying *their* sexuality. They were talking about *mine*. In other words, my gay family was outing me, despite the fact that I am not gay.

Where did they get this idea? Did they see me enjoying the penis cake a little too much? It was excellent cake!

Not only did I know myself to be not gay, but my heterosexuality was probably the only thing about myself in which I had any confidence at all. I'd known myself to be straight since the age of four, when I fell in love with a neighborhood girl my age named Sarah, who seduced me with the coquettish way she nibbled her carrot sticks. Although I could not have articulated at that age what I felt for Sarah, I remember it as a proto-sexual attraction, a thick emotional slurry warming my chest like hot cocoa. Young Sarah was only the first in a long string of girls I fell for throughout elementary school, middle school, and on into early high school, when Mom and Elaine informed me I was gay.

What they did not know was that, at the time of our talk, I had recently begun fingering a mopey latchkey girl from the neighborhood named Cathy. I don't even remember how it began between Cathy and me. Memories are, of course, unreliable, but I feel like one day she might have just said, "Hey, you want to come over and finger me?"

To which I would have replied, "Okay."

Every once in a while, I would visit her after school and we would plod upstairs to her room, where I would touch her and watch her react to my artless ministrations in a vague, disinterested way, as if she were hearing about them from a friend. My finger-banging skills may have been lacking, but they were without a doubt the result of heterosexual urges.

I wisely chose to withhold this information from Mom and Elaine during their living room intervention, which left me no credible defense against their accusation other than to get pissed off and sputter, "What are you talking about?"

"I just want you to know I still love you," Mom said.

What. The. Fucking. Fuck.

The most infuriating aspect about our heart-to-heart was their certainty. Fact: You are gay. As if I had no say in the matter. Some might point to this as evidence of the nefarious homosexual agenda that seeks to recruit children into their perverted lifestyle, but, in fact, the opposite was true: Their decision to confront me about my sexuality was partially in response to my mother's fervent desire that I *not* be gay. By the time they sat me down, it was only after my mother had resigned herself to the fact that she had a gay son. Of the two of us, *she* was the homophobe.

This took place during the height of the AIDS epidemic, an era before gay rights were a mainstream issue, before Madonna and Britney tongue-kissed on MTV. To be gay meant to risk being shunned, feared, and attacked. Our own home was the target of the occasional egging. Mom and Elaine kept their relationship as quiet as they could, absurdly masquerading as sisters, albeit sisters who looked about as much alike as Abbott and Costello. To have a gay son meant constant worry for his health and safety.

Years later, when I call to ask her about her memories of this conversation, she says, "I felt terrible because I didn't want you to be gay."

"Why?"

"It's a hard life. I wouldn't want it for any of my children. Plus I wanted grandchildren, goddamnit!"

"Well, this is the telephone conversation where I tell you I'm gay."

"I'll mark it down," she says.

To be fair, I can understand how my sexuality might have come under suspicion. The signs were everywhere. For one thing, at the age of nine, I declared my intention to devote my life to the theater, an institution not known for its robust heterosexual male population. Undeclared, however, was that much of my newfound interest in the theater had to do with a girl I'd fallen in love with while doing a play at summer camp. Mom heard "theater," and thought "gay." She also noticed the way I sometimes crossed my legs, and thought "gay." She saw that most of my friends were girls and thought "gay." In fact, she was a lot like my middle and high school classmates who noticed the same things and came to the same conclusion, albeit with fewer understanding words and more hard shoves into lockers.

Neither they nor Mom understood that I consciously cultivated a lot of my more "feminine" characteristics as a kind of informal protest against the New Jersey jock culture in which I found myself marooned. Guys in my hometown were expected to fall within a willfully stupid spectrum of masculinity that revolved around sports worship and farting. I didn't understand it and I didn't want to be part of it. The simple act of crossing my legs one on top of the other instead of ankle on knee was an act of quiet rebellion.

Back in the mid-'70s, when Mom and Elaine spent their weekends campaigning for the Equal Rights Amendment, they never quite realized that gender equality cuts both ways. The same protections for which they fought could also apply to men. No, we weren't subjected to workplace discrimination in the same way or harassed in the same way, but we, too, were vulnerable to cultural discrimination. A man had to conform to his role just as a woman was meant to conform to hers. While they struggled for women and girls to be free to become whomever they chose, it never occurred to them that some men and boys felt just as stifled. Boys like me. Nobody ever told me there were different ways to be male, so I felt forced to improvise, to play with masculine conventions and find ways to bend them to meet my own needs; they misinterpreted that improvisation as sexual confusion. Yes, most of my friends were girls, but not because I liked boys: It was because *I liked girls.*

As a father now myself, I am sensitive to all signs pointing toward the different directions my children may take. And I am sensitive to how gentleness in boys can be taken for evidence of incipient homosexuality. All the neighborhood parents gossip over which of the toddlers on the playground are going to grow up gay. Of course, now parents *want* their kids to be gay because having a gay kid has become a lifestyle, like eco-tourism. I try not to engage with this kind of tongue-wagging, because I know how it feels to be labeled as something you are not and because I know that boys are sometimes quiet and sometimes they eschew backyard football games in lieu of fingering the new girl down the street.

Our talk in the living room ended not long after it began. They told me I was gay. I told them I was not. We went back and forth like this a few times, with my bewilderment turning to embarrassment and then to anger. Within a few minutes I stormed off, screaming at them that they were crazy. That was the last time they raised the subject of my sexuality until an excruciating accusation during my senior year that I'd been having sex with my girlfriend in our house while Mom was at work, an accusation I vigorously and adamantly (and tearfully) denied, but which I will now cop to—yes, Mom, we were totally doing it while you were at work.

As transgressive as I felt my gay intervention to be, the event takes on a more complicated dimension when coupled with an event I learned of from Mom regarding her own sexual history, of which I knew nothing before I began interviewing her for this book. We'd never discussed that aspect of her life before because asking your mother about her sexual history is kind of like asking her to take off her top. It simply isn't done. But I have never been afraid to be creepy in the service of art, so I asked. And she told me.

Growing up, Mom never suspected herself to be gay. She's not even sure she knew what being gay meant. Nobody discussed homosexuality during Mom's formative years in the 1950s and early '60s. Having never been exposed to the idea, or even to the Indigo Girls, she had no reason to believe herself to be anything other than an ordinary Goody Two-shoes Chicago girl, an easy enough fiction to maintain during high school, when dating rituals were different than today. Back then, Mom says, couples didn't pair off and hook up the way they do today. Instead, teens went out in groups, presumably to sock hops and soda fountains and other pagan rituals from the mists of prehistory. All innocent Technicolor fun. Although I am sure some young ladies hoisted up their petticoats for whichever Marlon Brando wannabe smoldered in their direction, my prim mother-to-be did not knowingly consort with such hussies.

Her first inkling that something about her might be different occurred when she began babysitting for a young couple. Over time, she became close to the couple, spending more and more time with the mother because she preferred their house to hers. "I hated being at home," she says. "Hated it."

"Me too!" I want to say, but that seems unkind.

The couple's home became Mom's regular hangout. Alan, the husband, was a jeweler who worked late, so Mom and Alan's wife, Phyllis, would keep each other company. Nothing sexual ever happened between them, but Phyllis became increasingly important to Mom.

After graduation, Mom headed off to Indiana for college. While on break, she agreed to babysit for the couple so they could go away for a long weekend. I don't know what transpired during that long weekend, but upon Alan and Phyllis's return, Mom had what she calls "a nervous breakdown."

What does she mean? What happened? She tells me she has no memory of the details, for reasons that will soon become apparent. All she knows is that the couple called Mom's parents, who retrieved her from the house and brought her to the "hospital," where she was confined for six weeks.

There, Mom underwent an extensive course of electroshock treatments. Her parents, suspecting Mom's homosexuality, ordered the shock therapy without her consent. "They thought they could shock the gayness out of me," she says.

When I ask why her parents thought she was gay when she herself did not consider herself to be so, she has no answers. She doesn't remember. She doesn't remember much because the treatments "killed my memory from that point back."

Everything that occurred before her hospital stay, every memory, became a hazy blur. The treatment zapped away huge swaths of her childhood and adolescence, leaving her unsure, even today, of which are her actual memories and which are things people told her about herself after the fact. This is an uncommon, but well-documented, reaction to electroconvulsive therapy (ECT). Many patients experience short-term memory loss but recover. Some, like my mom, never regain their memories. In an op-ed piece written for the *Washington Post* in 2000, a nurse who had undergone ECT referred to her memory loss as "a rape of the soul."

The most common way to administer ECT is to first anesthetize the patient. Next, an electrode is placed near the temple. Finally, varying electrical charges of up to 450 volts are pumped directly into the brain, inducing seizure. Doctors don't understand exactly what happens during the seizure, but it seems to scramble the brain, the way you might smack a misbehaving television set hoping to reset the picture. The treatment is then repeated again and again and again, two or three times a week, for weeks at a time.

Although it sounds barbaric, ECT has been shown to have some positive effects on the treatment of depression. Nobody knows why, just as nobody knows why smacking the TV sometimes works. When it comes to altering homosexuality, though, ECT has no effect. Zero. Mom says the only things the treatment accomplished were fucking up both her memory and her feelings about her parents.

The only other "cure" for homosexuality in wide use at the time—and still in use by some "gay conversion clinics"—is called aversion therapy. If you've ever seen *A Clockwork Orange*, you already understand how this works. A patient is shown images of homosexual behavior while some painful physical sensation is applied to the body. This could be something as simple as ice applied to the hands while watching a gay couple holding hands; or, for more explicit sexual scenes, the treatment might involve applying heat or electricity directly to the genitals. Fun stuff. The idea is to teach the patient to associate homosexual behavior with pain, the same way I associate crème brûlée with throwing up because once I ate six of them in a row and then puked my guts out. Now I can't even look at the stuff. Aversion therapy, like ECT, does not change homosexuality. To my knowledge, crème brûlée therapy has never been tried. I doubt it would work, though, because the gays love those fancy French desserts.

I press Mom for more details: Why did her parents take such a drastic step? She says she cannot remember a thing about that time, but I have a theory:

While she was away at college, lonely and homesick, Mom's feelings for Phyllis ballooned from close friendship into romantic love. Upon Alan and Phyllis's return from their long weekend, Mom confessed her feelings to Phyllis in the overdramatic, flailing way of teenagers. She probably wept many tears, yelled many yells, threatened suicide, that sort of thing. The couple, fearing for Mom's safety, called her parents, who whisked her away to the loony bin and ordered her cured. Again, this is all speculation, but my theory would explain everything. (I also have an alternate theory of how the dinosaurs went extinct if any paleontological journals wish to contact me.)

Twenty years later, Mom replayed the same scene with me, shoving me into her old role of the confused teenager. Now was her big chance to correct the mistakes her parents had made. Instead of admonishing and punishing her gay kid, she offered unqualified love and support. A noble gesture—if I were gay. But I knew exactly which team I played for and, in fact, was already taking batting practice with the girl down the street.

It's weird that she did that, right? Weird that she reenacted a painful moment from her teen years with her own teenager? Or maybe it's just a bizarre example of the way families make the same mistakes generation after generation. For some families, it's booze or domestic abuse or early pregnancies. For mine, it's outing your kid.

I don't know who my kids are going to turn out to be yet—gay, straight, or whatever—but I'm grateful that I at least live in the first generation where any option is a good option. I just want them to find love; whichever genitals come with that love are irrelevant. Our bodies are confusing enough to ourselves without having other people telling us how they should behave or how we should use them. My only advice to them is simple: If they do have sex with their partners during high school, they should make sure to dry off their towels after showering together. It's a rookie mistake, and it's how my mom caught me.

CHAPTER TEN

Absurdly, I answered, "I'm fine"

Having just declared my heterosexuality, I will now supply ammunition for anybody who does not believe me: For a short while, I became obsessed with muscle magazines. No gayer periodical genre exists than those thick, glossy monthlies beguiling readers with promises to "get big." Splayed across their pages one will find endless photos of glistening, hairless giants grunting and sweating, their faces contorted into orgasmic rictuses. Often, they are pictured draped with chains or weighted down with iron plates. They are almost never photographed with women. The only thing separating these images from straight-up gay porn is a decided lack of mustaches.

My fascination began innocently enough with a casual magazine rack perusal during a prescription refill. There, amongst *People* and *Newsweek*, I discovered homoerotic titles like *Flex* and *Muscle*. At first, I flipped through them for the same reason I might look at *DDD Cup Magazine*: to gaze out in wonder toward the distant event horizon of human freakishness.

My initial reaction upon first seeing these steroid-addled cover boys was probably the same as most people's would be: disgust. Pro bodybuilders push the human form to unnatural dimensions, the results no less upsetting than those of Chinese foot binding. But the human mind is nothing if not adaptive, and as my eyes adjusted to these strange and swollen shapes, disgust turned to fascination, and fascination to respect.

I grew to love these self-described "freaks" and "beasts," men whose biceps literally have biceps, an additional bump on top of their regular bicep called a "bicep peak." Their names became as familiar to me as those of any movie star: Dexter Jackson, Lee Haney, Dorian Yates. To give you a sense of their size, consider a few of my measurements versus those of eight-time Mr. Olympia Ronnie Coleman.

	WAIST	CHEST	BICEP	CALVES	THIGHS
Me	32	39	12 1/2	14	20
Ronnie Coleman	36	58	24	22	36

In nearly all categories, there is nearly twice as much Ronnie Coleman as there is me. His thighs are bigger than my waist. His chest is bigger than my house. Plus, Ronnie Coleman, like all pro bodybuilders, is so very shiny. In addition to everything else, professional bodybuilders are the shiniest men in the world. I harbored no illusions that I would, or could, ever shine like those guys, but I figured I could make myself into a better, buffer, more Bruce Whitehall–esque me if I applied even 1 percent of the physical effort they did. So I joined a gym, my first.

That first summer morning in the gym, I attacked my exercises with an animalistic ferocity. Leg presses—BAM! Shoulder presses—SOCKO! Bench presses and squats—KAPOW! I concluded by ripping out a thousand (twelve) (weight-assisted) pull-ups. Sweaty and spent, I exploded onto the New York streets for a well-earned victory strut home. I remember the summer sun, overbright and painful, cutting into my eyes as I emerged from the sweatbox, already feeling my muscles expanding like sponges soaked in lava.

Then, while crossing the street, I had an unexpected thought: "You know what? I feel like sitting down for a moment."

One does not often develop an urge to have a sit-down on New York City sidewalks unless something is seriously wrong; after all, dog poo is usually the *least* offensive thing there. Head spinning, I plopped down onto the lip of the sidewalk to get myself sorted out. "No problem," I thought. "A little light-headedness is normal after fucking destroying a gym." Totally normal. Schwarzenegger once said he used to do sit-ups until he passed out, so I took my dizziness and shortness of breath as evidence that I was on the right track. I tried to stand. I sat back down, shoving my head between my legs to clear away the sparkles now detonating behind my eyelids. My heart began doing kangaroo kicks. Deep breathing did not help. Nor did the cooling sensation of brining in fresh sweat. I needed to lie down. "Normal?" I asked myself.

"Not normal," I answered, laying my full self out on the sidewalk. "I'm dying," I thought. "I am dying from a brain aneurysm on Twenty-Second Street between Park and Lex. I am dying on a street that doesn't even have a decent coffee shop."

This was before cell phones were in wide use, so I had no way of contacting Martha to bid her goodbye. Although we lived only a couple blocks away, she might as well have been on the dark side of the moon. My dying thoughts were of her, of the life we could have shared together, and of the fact that she had not yet paid her half of the rent. A minute or so passed before a woman stopped to ask if I was okay.

Absurdly, I answered, "I'm fine."

She didn't believe me. "Would you like me to call someone for you?"

"Would you mind calling my girlfriend?" This is what I think I said, but it may have come out more like: "Casneekahlmahgilmend?"

I gave the woman my telephone number, writing it down because

I did not trust my mouth to form digits. Somebody else stopped and offered to buy me a Gatorade, an offer I accepted with gratitude even though he bought me green Gatorade when I would have preferred red. Ask next time, asshole.

In a few moments, the woman returned from a pay phone, telling me Martha would be there soon. I heaved myself back into a seated position and sipped my (green) Gatorade. My head cleared. Martha ran up, panicked.

"What happened?" Martha asked.

"I think I overdid it at the gym," I answered.

"You need to be more careful!"

I shrugged with the cool insouciance of an X Gamer who'd just wrecked while attempting a 720 backside kickflip. Like, "Yeah, I crashed and burned but that's the price you pay for going to extremes." I did not tell her that I had been exercising with the weights on the lowest possible setting.

I never returned to that gym.

The next time I joined one occurred during a brief relocation to Los Angeles, which is the worst possible place to join a gym if you are somebody who looks as if he needs to join a gym, because nobody else there does. Hot bodies are LA's primary import. Good-looking people show up there by the thousands every day expecting to be paid for their beauty. It would be ridiculous were it not for the fact that many of them get their wish.

The sheer number of extraordinary-looking people in Los Angeles is disorienting at first. Everywhere you look is another perfectly symmetrical twentysomething. It is a city populated by people who look like what would happen if Abercrombie mated with Fitch. I would like to say I eventually became inured to all this physical beauty but I did not. Even when I visit now, years later, I am still just as gobsmacked walking around (or driving around, I should say, since walking is illegal in Los Angeles) as when I first arrived. Somehow the same exact beautiful twentysomethings are still there. Literally the same ones. They have not aged. They have not changed. They are the world's loveliest undead.

Because LA is a town filled with unemployed young people, its gorgeous denizens have nothing better to do than congregate at the gym. No actual exercise is conducted there because to do so would be redundant. After all, perfection has no need for improvement. Instead, the gym is a place to kvetch about show business, discuss various poolside barbecues, sip fresh-pressed wheatgrass smoothies. The gym is town hall and singles bar. It is beauty pageant ballroom. It is a lonely place for the scrawny and pale.

Alas, I am the scrawny and pale. Upon my entering, the front-desk Amazon would barely register my presence while swiping my membership card. Not even a "Have a good workout." Maybe it was for the best. After all, we both knew I would not be having a good workout. More apt would be if she had wished me a "grudging, slightly embarrassed workout." That was the sort of workout I would be having, and we both knew it. Once inside, my usual exercise routine was to skulk from machine to machine, avoiding eye contact with the demigods before me. Not that I needed to make any special effort to avoid their gaze: To them I was invisible.

My attendance declined over time, from four times a week, to three, to two, then finally to the occasional passing glance as I drove to In-N-Out Burger. For a while, I did see some modest improvement in my physique, but I never felt comfortable there among the better members of my species, and I eventually stopped going altogether, preferring to spend my time among my people, the schlubby Jews writing terrible screenplays at Starbucks.

My final attempt at regular weightlifting took place after I moved to my current town in the wilds of Connecticut. I picked this particular gym because membership came with three personal training sessions. I figured those free sessions would guarantee at least three trips to the gym because, although I hate working out, I hate losing out on free stuff more. The trainer promised to create for me an individualized workout regimen. All I had to do was follow it for a couple months, slap on some bronzer, and win Mr. Olympia.

I selected a female trainer out of fear that a male trainer would make fun of me. My fear turned out to be baseless. The female trainer I selected proved just as capable of making fun of me as any man.

At our first session, she led me around to the different machines we'd be working on, setting the load at what she thought I could handle, then gradually taking weight off when she realized I could not. This happened at every machine we visited: the leg press, shoulder press, chest thingy, back-of-the-leg thingy, other thingy. Maybe she knew the weights were too heavy and was subtly teasing me. But I doubt it. I think she found herself genuinely surprised every time I could not lift even the small amount of weight she selected. After an hour of lifting things and putting them down, punctuated by exasperated sighs from my trainer, I was freed from my labors and stumbled to my car, legs as pliable as willow branches.

We met again the following week. This time my trainer had a touch more sympathy for my delicate condition and smirked at my struggles less, even saying, "Nice job," after I completed my sets. But it wasn't a nice job. It was survival and whimpering. By week three, my soreness had abated somewhat, which made me push myself harder, which solicited more praise from the trainer. She pronounced me ready to tackle the gym on my own. I promised to make her proud. We shook hands. It hurt.

My first solo session ended about twenty minutes after it began when I found myself unable to stand while performing a squat. The squat is one of the major compound exercises wherein the worker-outer drapes a weighted barbell across his or her back, descends to a squatting position, then stands back up, a simple enough task to accomplish until one attempts to do it. Halfway through my second set, I descended to the squatting position and attempted to rise but found myself unable to do so. Trainers recommend having a spotter for occasions such as this, but I hadn't asked anybody to spot me because I am shy about asking muscular people for help owing to the fact that, when I was in high school, muscular people used to push me around and call me "faggot."

Finally, I did the only thing I could think of to do, which was to allow the barbell to roll along the top of my spine and onto the floor, compacting several vertebrae in the process. It landed with a metallic CLANK!, sending all eyes in my direction. Mortified, I tried to lift the barbell back onto the weight rack but found this task impossible as well. So I left the weight there on the floor and did what one does in such a situation—I ran away.

That was all the excuse I needed to never return to that gym. I kept telling myself I would, kept reassuring myself that I just needed to get back to work. But I didn't. Just like I didn't return to any of the gyms I have joined and quit over the years, letting the monthly charges accumulate, on average, about two years before removing myself from their membership rolls.

The worst moment of joining a gym is the moment when Martha notices I haven't been going for a couple weeks. "Are you going to go back to the gym?" she might ask in a tone she would probably describe as "curious," and which I would describe as "passive-aggressive."

The answer, of course, is no. No, I am not going back to the gym. Not ever. So I say, "Yes. I'm going back to the gym."

"Because if you're not going back to the gym, we should call them so they don't charge us every month."

"That would be the right thing to do if I weren't going back to the gym, but because I am, there's no need to call them."

"Because you always say you're going back and then you don't and we end up paying for the gym for two years even though you're not using it."

"I know that has happened in the past, but not this time."

Two years later, I call to get my name removed from the membership rolls.

My dream of looking like 1 percent of a professional bodybuilder is dead, just like my dreams of getting into shape by swimming, and my mountain biking dreams, and all the other dreams I have ever had of one day unearthing Bruce Whitehall from the sickly shell in which he is encased.

Maybe I could lower my expectations. Maybe I could just make small improvements on what I am instead of trying to make myself into something I will never be.

I had to try *something*, but what? Team sports were out because that would involve interacting with other people. I mean, what was I going to do? Join a team and get to know people and maybe go out for drinks afterward to recount some hilarious event that had just transpired on the field of play and wind up with a bunch of new friends bound together by the camaraderie that unites men who have struggled together to achieve some arduous goal? How stupid would that be? No, whatever I decided to do had to be a solitary activity, one that required no expensive equipment or lessons or fixed schedules. Something I could do at my own pace in my own time, preferably something I already knew how to do. Really, there was only one sport left. But it was a sport that filled me with dread and fear. Even so, I had to try. So I went for a run.

It sucked.

CHAPTER ELEVEN

My arrogance is stronger than my brain

There are many running books out there—dozens, maybe hundreds—that will inform the reader on all manner of running topics: footwear, training programs, proper form, diet, and so on. But none of them will tell you running's primary attribute, which is that it sucks. Running advocates focus on the sport's non-sucky elements, the most cited being the "runner's high," that mystical endorphin rush runners experience when they have pushed themselves into a blissful state of forgetting the fact that they are running. I, too, have experienced the runner's high. I get it every time I stop.

There are two reasons running sucks. The first is because it's boring. Putting foot in front of foot for an hour or more at a time is tedious, even when listening to music or podcasts or books on tape or motivational speakers or TED talks or the sound of the woods or any of the other distractions I have used to pass the time.

The runner is encouraged to experience the outdoors, to take in its bounty, to feel the wind against his face and know he is one with his environment. The runner is asked to launch himself through space by the volition of his own feet, to propel himself across its vast and wondrous terrain and to feel himself to be master of his own destiny as he surveys the world, arms akimbo, from the top of its mountains, mountains he has summited through the application of willpower alone, the diligent repetition of footstep following footstep leading, incredibly—inevitably—to glory. It sounds noble, and I suppose it is, in the way that suffering can become ennobling, particularly when somebody else is doing the suffering.

Some people use running to detach themselves from the workaday world's unceasing thrum. For those hours on the road or trail, they may forgo electronic communication in favor of communion with the natural world. That's fine for them, I guess, but the reason millions of people prefer the electronic world to the natural one is because the electronic world has funny videos of cats playing the piano, and the natural world does not.

The second reason running sucks is because it hurts. Sometimes it hurts your knees or your lower back or your feet. In my case, it hurts all of the above, plus my right shoulder, which seems like an odd place for running to hurt, but it is the location of my most frequent discomfort, due to my scoliosis.

Whether or not I actually have scoliosis has been a matter of some confusion to me for more than thirty years. One day when I was in fifth grade, our entire class got called down to the nurse's office for scoliosis tests. Per state law, all fifth graders were required to go through this drill. We lined up outside the nurse's station and were brought inside one at a time. When it was my turn, she told me to bend over and touch my toes, which I did. As I stood, she ran her fingers over my spine and said, "You have scoliosis."

Oh no.

Scoliosis was bad. I knew this because I had already read the Judy Blume book *Deenie*, about a girl with scoliosis who has to wear a back brace. She worries that the brace will crater her nascent love life. Who will ever feel her up over a back brace? It would be like going to second base with C-3PO. In the end, Deenie wears the brace and also finds love. Good news for her, but even at the age of ten, I understood that having scoliosis would brand me a freak. Even as it straightened my spine, I knew the brace would twist my social life into something ugly and deformed. Scoliosis was a death sentence. Worse, it was a girl's disease.

Girls are diagnosed with scoliosis at a ratio of 10:1. How had I, already pegged as somewhat less masculine than the other boys, developed a girl's disease? I could see my already dim prospects for social success in middle school now winking out entirely.

I left the nurse's office with my diagnosis, eyes downcast, my future self being fitted for a cumbersome metal cage, all hopes of tongue-kissing forever lost. When I got home, I did not mention the exam to Mom. She would find out when the school called.

But then, a mysterious thing happened. Or, rather, didn't happen. The school never called. A day went by. Then a week. No telephone call. Nothing. They never even gave me one of those ominous sealed envelopes to bring home for signature. After a month, it became clear they never would. I felt thrilled and terrified. Should I say something? Should I alert Mom to my curvature of the spine, which, left untreated, would leave my vertebrae as tangled as our kitchen telephone cord? Or should I just keep my mouth shut, knowing I was trading the short-term gain of possibly making out with somebody against the future risk of becoming a troll who lives under a bridge? The decision was easy: I kept my mouth shut. Within a year, I stuck my tongue in Wendy Jamieson's mouth. It was gross.

I grew up. I do not live under a bridge. To my layman's eye, my spine appears more or less straight, although I have noticed that my right shoulder does ride a bit higher than my left, which I assume is what produces that uncomfortable ache in my shoulder while running. I've done everything I can think of to do to lessen the pain, although the only thing I can think to do is roll my shoulder around a few times, which does little to offset my discomfort but does produce a series of satisfying clicks. How do you spell "s-c-o-l-i-o-s-i-s" in Morse code?

Every now and again, I wonder what happened. Once the nurse gives you a scoliosis diagnosis, isn't she supposed to follow up? Aren't the school authorities supposed to sound the scoliosis bell? Call in one of those cool medevac helicopters? Was the nurse just messing with me that day? If so, I have to admit, that's a pretty good practical joke.

There are other pains associated with running. Many of them. This is normal. In fact, according to the American Academy of Physical Medicine and Rehabilitation, 70 percent of all runners can expect to become injured each year. Seventy percent! Those are Ebola numbers! Running is to the body what demolition derby is to the automobile. Why begin an activity that you can predict with near certainty will leave you unable to continue said activity in the not-too-distant future? It seems counterintuitive unless you consider that the injury will give you permission to stop.

Yet, here I was, ready to start.

Choosing running wasn't entirely random. I'd been intrigued with distance running dating back to freshman year of high school, when I attended an informational meeting about joining the cross-country team, thinking I needed to boost my high school extracurricular résumé in anticipation of dropping out of college a couple years later.

We were a shabby, sallow group at that sparsely attended meeting. None of us very athletic looking. None of us popular. The coach wore a saggy tracksuit, his mustache an unaccomplished strip of fuzz. He sat at the end of a lunch table and laid out his expectations for the upcoming season. These expectations had something to do with being "competitive," although the way he said "competitive" made me think he expected us to do a lot of losing. Then he handed out mimeographed training schedules, detailing the running regimen we were to follow over the summer months. Running? Over the summer? I took one look at the ditto with its carefully prescribed mileage plans and muttered to myself a quiet "Fuck this."

You may ask, if I wasn't prepared to, you know, *run*, why did I attend a meeting for the cross-country team? After all, running is pretty much all they do. I guess I thought the actual running part wouldn't start until school resumed, when we would head out together, as one, on some crisp autumn day, perhaps in matching cardigan sweaters, maybe puffing from handsome meerschaum pipes as we jogged along. We would be like a pack of nattily attired zebras trotting the savanna. It never occurred to me that there would be summer running, which would conflict with my already-scheduled summer sleeping, summer television watching, and summer complaining that I had nothing to do. Seeing all that mileage charted in unyielding columns and rows—three miles one day, five the next—frightened me. I didn't even know if I could run *one* mile, let alone multiples of the things. Once I factored in the possibility that a carload of football players might see me, panting along the road in short shorts, I became dissuaded. After all, a herd of zebras is majestic. A solitary zebra is prey. No, running would have to wait. Perhaps forever.

Forever lasted until my freshman year of college at NYU, when my new roommate Dan suggested we take a run together. Dan was an amiable kid from upstate New York who had been on his high school track team, and who dreamed of becoming a foot doctor, which struck me as a bizarre career aspiration. What eighteen-year-old wants to be a podiatrist? Didn't he know that feet are disgusting? Imagine having to use the word *bunion* on a daily basis. In the politest possible terms, I asked him how he came to choose that particular profession: "That's fucking gross," I said.

Dan explained that he'd developed an interest in feet during his varsity running days, and by the way, would I be interested in taking a run with him? Dan ran all the time, sometimes twice a day. He often asked if I'd like to join him. I kept putting him off. "Maybe another time," I'd say.

Why didn't I just say no, as in "no other time"? That would have ended his requests. I think part of me wanted to test my mettle against Dan, to see how I stacked up against my track star roommate. I didn't expect to beat him in a footrace or anything, but I figured I could probably hold my own. Why did I think this? Because my arrogance is stronger than my brain.

Finally, a couple months after we settled in together, I agreed to go for a run with Dan. I don't even think I had anything to run in. Maybe some sweats, a T-shirt, and a pair of beat-up Converse. Dan had nylon shorts, tiny socks, running shoes. He looked like an athlete. I looked like a guy who recycles cans.

We lived on the edge of Washington Square Park, and our plan was to run through the park, up Fifth Avenue, cross somewhere in Midtown, then make our way back down Broadway toward home, a gentle and flat route, probably no more than two and a half or three miles. "No problem," methought, imagining a brisk and tidy scamper through our fair city. I pictured us chatting and laughing as we zipped along the sidewalks, dodging pedestrians, jumping over taxicabs. We emerged from our dorm, windmilled our arms, stretched out our hammies, and took off.

Dan set a murderous pace, closer to a sprint than a jog, leaving me exhausted by the time we crossed beneath the triumphal stone arch marking the park's entrance. I stopped, bent over at the waist, lungs collapsed. We'd gone maybe two hundred yards.

"Come on!" Dan barked, not even winded. He jogged in place, waiting for me to collect myself. Dan's eyes were hard to read, but I saw something new in them, something approaching disgust. "Come on!" he said again, challenging me to continue.

"I can't," I answered, wheezing.

He gave me a final, withering appraisal before dashing up Fifth

Avenue, his heels kicking high behind him. I watched him disappear into a thicket of slow-motion New Yorkers, knowing he was experiencing a primal triumph over me, the ancient dominance of alpha male over omega, the natural order of all things confirmed. After losing sight of Dan, I stood up and trudged back to our dorm room. Dan never again asked me to go running with him. There was no need. He had proven his point; he was the better man. We didn't room together sophomore year.

It would be another twenty years before I committed to running in a serious way, and only after I had eliminated every other physical activity I could think to do. If I could not swim or mountain bike or lift weights or play team sports or bull ride or luge, I would run. I knew running would hurt, and I knew it would suck, but I wanted it for me. Part of me also wanted it for Mom. As her mobility declined, my own sedentary lifestyle began to feel offensive. How could I justify spending my time lying on the couch for hours on end when I knew she would have given anything to be able to move about without hindrance? I resolved to get moving. At least one of us should stand on top of mountains, arms akimbo, surveying the world. And if mountains seemed too high, then perhaps hills. Or an oversized speed bump. At least one of us should be out of doors, planting foot in front of foot, pretending to enjoy nature. Our lives are short and growing shorter all the time. Maybe running could beat back death a little bit. Or, barring that, maybe it would at least make me yearn for death's sweet release if it sucked as much as I thought it would.

CHAPTER TWELVE

There are no good prizes

First of all, it's not a race. They can call it a race if they want, but the fact of the matter is, 99 percent of all participants are not trying to win. They're trying to survive. No recreational road race is truly a race, because races demand competition, and in these endeavors there is practically none. Most people just want to finish the damn thing. Sure, there's always a few folks at the head of the pack trying to win, but those people are dickheads. I mean, what does it really gain you in life to be able to say, "I won the St. Mary's Autumn Harvest 10K Road Race"?

Also, there are no good prizes. Real races would have good prizes. Cash, say. At these races, every single person who finishes the race receives a cheap medal to hang around their neck. Once they get home, the medal goes into a drawer along with all the other "prizes" they "won" for simply doing what they signed up to do in the first place.

So it's not a race, but there's probably no better name for what these events actually are. "Fun run" doesn't quite cover it either, because they're not that much fun, at least in the way I define fun, which can cover a wide range of undertakings but never includes any activity I am trying to bring to an end as quickly as possible.

Some races are described by their distances, as in the Waterloo Half Marathon. That's a good name because it tells you where the race is and how far the race goes. There's no need to jazz it up any further. If you are running a distance greater than from your front porch to the mailbox, you are already committed enough that you don't need some creative race director to make it sound more exciting. Leafing through the back pages of *Runner's World* magazine, however, it's clear a lot of these directors disagree. There's the Shamrock Shuffle, the Color Me Rad novelty race, the Hot Chocolate 15K, the Food Fight 5K, the Cherry Creek Sneak, Rock the Block, and the Viking Assault. (Granted, the Viking Assault actually does sound pretty cool.) But whatever they are called, and whatever gimmicks organizers use to make them seem like more than they are, road races all boil down to the same simple idea: Mark off a starting line and a finish line, then run between the two.

Some of these distances can get stupid. For years, people thought marathoners were nuts. The idea of running twenty-six (point two, as marathoners invariably point out) miles seemed insane. But as more and more people began participating in marathons, the distance lost some of its mystique. The marathon, commemorating the distance traveled by the Greek messenger Pheidippides, who allegedly *died* after running it, has become humdrum. This has paved the way for the "ultramarathon," or "ultra." Typical ultra distances are fifty or even a hundred miles. Some go two hundred miles or more. One annual run is called the Self-Transcendence 3100 Mile Race, which is remarkable not only for its distance, but for the fact that the entire event takes place over sixty days on a single, half-mile block in Queens, New York. Runners literally spend two months running in circles. The record is held by Suprabha Beckjord, who finished the race in forty-nine days, fourteen hours, thirty minutes, and fifty-four seconds. His prize? A small bouquet.

I chose a more modest distance for my first race, a 10K, or six miles, which seemed ambitious but doable. I registered for the event as soon as I started running, figuring I could use a tangible goal to work toward. Once I commit to something, I commit—at least until I quit, which can happen at any time.

I'd never trained for an athletic competition before. The closest I'd come was memorizing a blackjack chart. The thought of actually adhering to a training regimen exhilarated and frightened me. Here I was, a middle-aged man attempting something new, something the younger and fitter teenage runner in me had shied away from, something my now-infirm mother would never be able to do, something I hoped would inspire my children to get off their own asses.

I downloaded a training plan from a running site, and there, laid out in the same neat columns and rows I'd seen at the cross-country informational meeting years before, were numbers. Many, many numbers. Each number represented how many miles I would be running on any given day. It was a lot of miles. Day by day, though, the numbers didn't seem too daunting. The chart had me starting at only two miles, which didn't sound so hard. After all, two miles is only one more than one mile, and one mile is only one more than zero miles. I had already mastered the zero-mile distance, so I just needed to run what I'd already been running, plus two. Surely I could do that.

As it happens, I could not. The first time I tried, the distance of even a single mile amazed me. When zipping along in a car, a mile seems like the smallest denomination of distance; anything under a mile is hardly worth driving at all. But by foot, a mile is something else entirely. For the out of shape and listless, it is the stuff of Lewis and Clark, an endless, almost insurmountable length: 5,280 feet. If you were to lay all those feet end to end, it would stretch for an entire mile! While jogging on the road the first time, I kept checking the GPS on my phone to find out how far I'd run. What I thought should be a mile turned out to be about a tenth of a mile. Had they increased the length of miles since I was a kid?

Incredibly, the second mile was even longer than the first.

I got through that first training session only after taking frequent walking breaks and allowing myself to drift along on a steady stream of muttered curses. It's not that the distance itself was so draining, but my body was unaccustomed to doing anything more strenuous than raising itself from one couch and shuffling to another. My sweat glands, relieved to finally have something to do, deluged me. By the time I dragged myself home, I looked like I'd been dropped in a carnival dunk tank. Pathetic. One day was enough running for me. I decided to stop.

But I did not stop. I wanted to. I really, really wanted to. The next morning, competing voices screamed at me from inside my head. "Go out and run!" said one.

"Stay home and sleep!" said the other.

"Run!"

"Tostitos!"

I've never understood the ability that people have to hold opposing voices in their minds. There's one telling me I need to get out and exercise, the other reminding me that I haven't seen that cool documentary about whale abuse that I really should sit down and watch, preferably while stuffing my face. The only reason I hadn't seen the documentary to that point was that I'd rather do anything than watch a movie about whale abuse, anything that is, except run. And then there's a third voice, the "me," listening to the other me's, trying to decide what to do. Who are these voices, and which is my authentic self?

Scientists have been working on this question for decades. What they've learned so far is that the "inner speech" we have in our heads physiologically mimics the "external speech" we use when speaking. Weirdly, even our larynxes make little vibrations similar to those made while speaking when we have these thoughts. It turns out that all these disparate voices are manifestations of brain processes that compare, judge, weigh evidence, and make decisions. The voices we "hear" are simply the process our minds use to translate these competing thoughts into ideas we can understand on a conscious level. So, when we hear ourselves "talking" to ourselves, what we are hearing is akin to a computer reading text to us. At least I think that's a decent analogy, but maybe I've gotten it totally wrong. My inner critic is telling me that's a terrible comparison and that I'm an idiot.

All of this raises the question: When my mom heard her own Voice, a voice unlike any she had ever heard, what exactly was she hearing? Some omnipotent deity or a manifestation of calm her own body generated to comfort her in a time of stress? I choose to think it was God, because the voice turned out to be correct. And also because it makes a much better story. And also because it kind of makes my mother holy, and therefore me holy by extension.

So, despite my internal tabernacle chorus singing "I don't want to," I got my butt out the door that second day and ran. And again the day after that. After the first couple weeks, two miles no longer seemed quite so horrific. Soon I could jog the entire distance without any walk breaks. Then I expanded my range. Three- and four-mile jogs became possible, then doable, then done. The process was slow, and often ended with me back at my home collapsed on the grass trying to squeeze any extra oxygen from the air, but those times grew less frequent and eventually only occurred after I challenged myself to beat my personal bests at various distances. If I just took it slow, I found I could run for a good long while without any great suffering. Except for the pain in my scoliosis shoulder. And lower back. And knees. And shins.

I ate better. Not perfectly, but better. No more garbage cereals for breakfast. Just a post-run protein shake. Lunch might consist of a salad and a turkey burger. I cut down on late-night pretzel binges.

Weight started to slide off like snow from a metal roof. A few pounds, nothing amazing. But I felt better.

Did I grow to enjoy running? In moments, yes. Although I belittled the runner's high earlier, the truth is, I did experience the occasional blissed-out happy trance while jogging along to some funky jam on my iPod. Bouncing through the woods could produce a flash of happiness, a little burst of joy punctuating my runs. The high never lasted more than a quarter mile or so, but neither did the misery. My general mood during these runs leveled out somewhere between anxious and smug. Anxious because running can get a little worrisome if you're too hot or too far from home. Smug because every time a car passed me on the road, I allowed myself to think, "I'm better than you." And if believing yourself to be superior to the sedentary isn't the ultimate point of any physical activity, I don't know what is.

Race day finally arrived, a crisp October morning three months after I began training. When leaving home that morning, I instructed Martha and the kids to meet me at the finish line a little under an hour after I began. I wanted the kids to see me finish, not so much for my own ego, although that definitely played a part, but because I thought it important that they see their father actually doing something physically demanding in the hopes that it would, someday, inspire them to take similar action for their own health and well-being. Role models are important, and I wanted to be one for them. Don't get me wrong—they already admire the hell out of me—but I wanted to give them something else about their father to hold in awe.

I wore my lucky black jogging shorts and neon yellow "technical shirt." I have no idea what makes a shirt technically technical, but I believe it has something to do with wicking and/or fluorescence. After arriving at the church where the race would begin, I signed in, affixing my number 9 race bib to my torso with safety pins and collecting my souvenir T-shirt, which I scoffed at because it was non-technical. Then I walked outside to mingle with the others before the race. About a hundred and fifty runners congregated in the frosty air, stretching their hammies and quads, jumping in place, elevating their knees to chest height, executing quick warm-up sprints up and down the asphalt. I did not want to give myself away as a novice so I joined them in their exertions, even though I normally do very little stretching when running, because I'd read that stretching is overrated and also because it hurts.

As race time approached, we shepherded ourselves to the starting line, faster runners in front, slower runners like myself at the rear. I'd read that I should run my own race at my own pace, and try not to let the emotions of the moment force me into a quicker pace than for what I had trained. It seemed like sound advice. No sense in wringing myself out during my first race. My only goal was to complete the six miles in an unhurried hour. Somebody shot off a starter's gun, and I started running as fast as I could.

Despite my best intentions to do otherwise, I definitely got swept up in the moment and began the run at a much faster clip than I'd intended. The first bit was downhill, anyway, so I could do that part fast, then slow down to my regular pace and still beat my hour goal. As the downhill section flattened out, however, I did not slow my pace, because I found myself running beside a twelve-year-old girl and she did not slow hers. How could I slow down if she did not? Fortunately, owing to her superior athleticism, she pulled way ahead of me and I was able to relax my stride a bit in time for the big uphill we'd been warned about. The wilds of Connecticut are a hilly place, and I'd trained on hills already, but I still found this particular climb a bit dispiriting. It wasn't that steep, but it seemed to go on forever. Already, some of my competitors were slowing to a walk. Not me. No, this was a running race and I would run the damned thing even if it killed me. I made it to the hilltop without too much trouble and settled into an easy groove for the first half of the race, which looped me back to the church, where the 5K participants dropped out, leaving us hard-core 10K runners to do the course again.

By lap two, I found myself flagging a bit, but I was buoyed by thoughts of my kids seeing me cross the finish line, arms raised in triumph, 1976 Bruce Jenner hair flapping behind me. (Never mind that I did not have 1976 Bruce Jenner hair; my hair, as I have said, more closely approximated 1999 Bruce Willis hair.) As far as pace, I wasn't doing too badly. True, the front-runners had already finished by the time I began my second lap. True, my breath was a touch ragged, and yes, many of the runners traveling at my pace were overweight women several years my senior. And it galls me to admit, many of those same runners were offering me encouragement instead of the other way around, because I apparently looked as though I needed additional encouragement. None of that could ruin my mood as I conquered the hill for a second time and glided through the rolling suburban streets.

As I reached the final mile or so, I spotted a couple of older women just ahead of me: one thin, one stout. I could pass them. I knew I could pass them. I picked up my pace a bit, reeling them toward me one yard at a time. Maybe they heard my wheezing behind them, I don't know, but they picked up their pace too, keeping themselves just out of reach. I sped up again, as did they. I could get no closer than twenty yards, but kept pushing myself. I resolved to pass them, and in doing so, destroy them. I would destroy those two mommies.

I finally blew by them as we raced down the big hill again, not even offering a conciliatory sidelong glance as I sped past. Going downhill is actually harder than going up because of the terrible pounding it gives your legs. It hurts, particularly after already having run several miles. By the time I reached the bottom, my legs felt as though they'd been sunk in lead, and it wasn't long before the two mommies passed me right back, casually chatting to each other as they did so. Chatting! Casually! A gentle breeze carried them away from me and out of sight.

At least I was in the homestretch, less than half a mile from my triumph. I resolved to get myself together for that last little bit, to look confident and cool as I crossed the finish line, to give my kids a picture-perfect ending they could carry around in their mental wallets for the rest of their lives. Their father: young, athletic, the picture of health and virility. As I neared the church, volunteers exhorted me to "finish strong!" I waved them off, as if to say, "I do not need your exhortations, volunteers. The looks of adulation I will find on my blessed offspring are all the motivation I need."

Spectators clapped for me as I wound my way up the church driveway to the finish line. I could see a clock clicking off the seconds. I was five minutes ahead of pace! I was going to set a personal record in front of my family! The announcer congratulated each runner as they finished. I raised my arms as he said, "Number nine finishing in fifty-five minutes, twenty-three seconds." I'd done it. I'd run my race. I'd beat my goal time. I was a hero. Now to collect congratulatory hugs from my wife and kids. Who were not there.

Slowing to a walk, I looked around the finish area. No wife and kids. I walked to the aid station and orange-slice-distribution center. No wife and kids. I couldn't understand. Where were they? Somebody put a medal around my neck. I thanked them and kept searching for my family. Were they along the race route somewhere? I walked around, heart pounding, out of breath. No. Had they not come? It seemed like maybe they hadn't come at all. My heart fell into my running shoes.

Why hadn't they come?

I stumbled around for several more minutes, scanning faces, and, not finding theirs, decided to go home. As I dragged my feet to the car, I saw Martha and the kids approaching. They'd just arrived.

"Did you finish already?" Martha asked.

I couldn't even answer I was so upset.

"You said to come about an hour after the start."

I nodded and looked at the digital clock, still ticking off seconds as the last stragglers crossed the finish line. It was well past an hour after the start. I gave the kids each a hug and mumbled something about leaving.

"But we just got here," said my daughter.

"Daddy's mad at me," answered Martha.

"I'm not mad," I said.

I got into my car and drove off, furious. Didn't she understand how important this was to me? That I'd been training for months? That I wanted the kids to see me finish something, to inspire them? Despondent and hurt, I stomped upstairs, ignoring Martha for the rest of the day despite her repeated apologies. The medal got thrown into a cigar box, the race bib shoved into a sweater cubby.

Around dinnertime I started to calm down a bit. After all, was it really that big a deal? So I ran a race. It wasn't even a long race. As I said before, it wasn't even a race. Six miles. That's not even a quarter marathon. What did I really have to be upset about? Was this maybe about me wanting exorbitant praise for doing something that's not that hard? Maybe. But then again, I'd just completed something I didn't know I could even do a couple months before. I didn't think it was wrong to want my family there to witness my accomplishment, however small. After all, I go to my kids' musical recitals, and those are terrible.

Families sometimes hurt each other. That's all there is to it. Martha didn't intend to let me down. She was late, that's all. Was I going to hold it over her head for the rest of our lives? Of course not. I would forgive her and then, a few years later, write about it in a book the way any good husband would.

Ultimately, the race didn't matter. What mattered was getting out on the road. Using my body. Not being a slug. Plus, I'd gotten a gift that wouldn't end with the race. I was a runner now! Running had become an integral part of my life. I was eating better, sleeping better, feeling better. That was the true gift. Not the congratulations, not the medal. It was those days outdoors, small pains and all. It was the sensation of autumn air moving across my face, just as I'd imagined it sitting at the cross-country informational meeting years before; it was the sting of cold water on my feet after sloshing through a puddle, my shadow chasing me across the miles. Also, it was the permission I gave myself to eat as much post-run ice cream as I wanted, because surely an elite athlete such as myself needed those extra calories. It wasn't true, of course, but I was already lying to myself about enjoying running, so why stop now?

CHAPTER THIRTEEN

Fill it with premium

Mom cannot remember if she had her hip replaced in between or after her two hernia operations. You know things have gotten bad when you can no longer remember how many surgeries you've had, or the order in which they happened. What we both remember is the intense pain she was experiencing around this time, so bad that each step left her gasping for air, making it nearly impossible for her to walk. An examination revealed the radiation had caused her left hip to, in her words, "crumble." Essentially, she no longer had a hip. One upside of her condition was that her surgeons "loved it."

She says: "They were so excited when they saw me afterward because they didn't expect it to be so bad and they rarely get to operate on one so bad. So they were thrilled. I told them I was very happy for them."

From the operation, she went to rehab. "One of the worst experiences of my life." This from a woman who had electricity zapped through her brain for five weeks. Finally, they released her back into the Florida swamps, where she recuperated. But the pain did not end with the new hip. If anything, it grew worse.

Pain became an unyielding, obtrusive force in Mom's life. In addition to the hip pain, she began experiencing persistent back pain, which made it difficult for her to sit in one position for more than a few minutes. Turns out she has an "unstable spinal column." Whatever supportive tissue her spinal column once had to keep her ambulatory and upright has been worn away, so now her spine has the structural integrity of a Jenga tower.

She cannot walk more than a few steps without the pain stopping her. Consultations with doctors yield no solutions. Because of her age and health history, she is not a candidate for reparative surgery, which involves plates and screws and some of those chip clips used to keep pretzels fresh in the bag. In the end, the doctors all tell her the same thing: Her condition is degenerative, inoperable, and eventually she will be confined to a wheelchair. In the meantime, pain is making life unbearable. A friend suggests marijuana.

"You tried marijuana?" I ask.

"Mm-hm," she says, pleased with herself.

"Was that your first time?"

"Oh no," she says offhandedly, as if it were Cheech & Chong & Jill.

I know being shocked to discover that your parents have tried drugs is passé, but for some reason, the thought of my utterly square mother toking up causes me greater mental distress than anything else she's told me. I guess it's like that dream where you discover a whole other room in your home you never knew existed. In this case, the new room is a dank, paneled basement from the '70s.

"I tried pot a couple times," she says, "but I could never really get high on it."

Me too! I have also tried marijuana a couple (around thirty) times, finally giving up on it after I came to the conclusion that I would never get it to work right. Either I ended up unconscious, which was what happened the first time, or I just stood around listening to other people giggle. Which is such a shame, because weed seems to me like the perfect drug: non-injectable, easily obtainable, and available in brownie form. If only I could nail down the part where it's an enjoyable, mildly narcotic experience and not a cotton-mouthed descent into gripping paranoia.

After giving up on weed, Mom and Sandy sought out a pain management specialist. They found one she now calls Dr. Schmuck.

They had unwittingly stumbled across a quack who began prescribing Mom megadoses of OxyContin, otherwise known as "hillbilly heroin," which, ever the good patient, she took as ordered. Every few weeks, they returned to the doctor's office where, she says, he cracked a couple jokes, refilled her prescription, and charged her several hundred dollars for the privilege of receiving suicidal doses of opiates.

"I found out later I was on extremely high, extremely dangerous doses of OxyContin. It was costing us upward of two thousand dollars a month. It was horrible. It got to the point where it was, 'Do I take the OxyContin or do we eat?'"

Although Mom kept Eric and me informed of what was going on with her during this period, I guess I didn't quite realize until now how dire things had become financially. Or, more likely, I knew but chose to ignore it because I did not want to send her money. Because I am a horrible son.

Money is an unacknowledged point of bitterness and contention between Mom and myself. The issue is complicated and laden with old hurts, so I will try to explain my side of it as fairly as I can, with the full understanding that, at some point, Mom will read this and get pissed at me.

You know how some people from poor families say, "We never had any money but never felt poor because we had love"? I always felt the opposite. "We never had any money and we always felt poor because our home life was a shit show." Mom and Dad fought over it, and their drawn-out divorce cost them both plenty of it. Afterward, I heard what seemed like daily litanies about child support and alimony and the cost of school clothes, as well as the cost of everything else.

Then, when Elaine and Mom set up house together, they expressed the desire to become a family, but it was a lie from the get-go. I remember loud fights between them over grocery bills, for example, with Elaine claiming she should owe less because she had only had one kid. In those moments, I distinctly felt like the idea of our ever being a family was a farce. I was probably about eight years old, and I can tell you from experience that no eight-year-old wants to hear that he costs too much. Their money arguments extended to every niggling aspect of the household, provoking countless fights, stony silences, and tearful remonstrations. Money was our home's perpetual emotion machine.

When I was around thirteen, Mom and Elaine decided to start a business together, a stationery and gift store. Mom and Elaine asked to borrow five thousand dollars from the life insurance money I'd received after Dad died. Eric and I had both elected to take much less than our equal share to ensure that Susan would always have enough. Our shares of the money were supposed to last long enough to see us through college, and five thousand dollars from that sum was a not insignificant amount.

"What if the business fails?" I asked Elaine, which seemed to me to be the kind of prudent question any investor would ask. Elaine didn't see it that way. She grew furious and screamed at me, causing a huge stink. I never gave them permission to take the money, but they did anyway.

The store failed while we boys were at college. Mom and Elaine ditched New Jersey, absconding to Florida in the middle of the night, leaving our home to the bank. A few years after that, they broke up, and Mom sank into a deep depression, during which she hibernated and did not work. How did she manage to live? I don't know, but if I had to guess, I would surmise she borrowed money from Susan's account, money she had no way of repaying. This is a subject that has never come up between us and probably never will. I am not going to ask her about it because I do not want to hear the answer and also because I am afraid.

As it happens, although her medication bills remained high, they lowered considerably once the feds started closing in on Dr. Schmuck. South Florida had become a hotbed of prescription abuse due to the population of vulnerable elderly people and the presence of Rush Limbaugh. The government began cracking down on questionable medical practices, and one week Dr. Schmuck announced to Mom and Sandy that he would be shutting down his practice effective immediately. Before he disappeared to Argentina or wherever quacks fly south to in times of trouble, he did refer Mom to a different pain specialist, who took one look at Mom's chart and told her she was lucky to be alive. She said Dr. Schmuck had basically turned Mom into a heroin addict, which, while tragic, did give my mother some much-needed street cred. The first step would be to wean her off pain pills, a process the doctor warned would be difficult. To Mom's surprise, though, quitting the OxyContin gave her no trouble at all, which led to the obvious question: What happened to all the extra pills, and could I have them?

To replace the OxyContin, her new doctor surgically implanted a pain pump, which alleviates the worst of her pain, allowing her to function again. So now, instead of going to Dr. Feelgood every couple of weeks, she visits her new doctor every few months to get her pump refilled with a pupu platter of morphine, Dilaudid, fentanyl, and whatever opiates are on sale at Costco that week. The pain is still there, and her spine is so badly misaligned that when she sits on the electric scooter she now needs to get around, she looks like a question mark. But at least she has enough pain-free moments that life is again tolerable.

(No word on whether or not she says, "Fill it with premium," when she gets the pain pump refilled, the way I would. I would do this every single time. And it would never, ever get old.)

In the end, I did start giving Mom money because she needs it and I am her son and I love her. And because I felt so fucking guilty. The right thing to do would have been to just offer it, but I didn't do the right thing. Instead, I waited for her to ask for help, which makes me feel sick every time I think about it, because I know how hard it must have been for her. Once I did start giving, I wanted to be glad to do it, but was not. These are the sorts of thoughts that tumble through the brain when running, and in those moments, it becomes clear that at least half of running's purpose is trying to run away.

Families are meant to take care of each other, even when it feels unfair. It's not fair that Mom got sick. It's not fair that she and Sandy only had a couple healthy years together beforehand. Nor is it fair that Mom couldn't get on Sandy's health insurance plan for years because, you know, gay. None of it is fair.

So how do you deal with unfairness? Pain management. We're all pain management patients in one way or another. My preferred method is pills of any size, shape, or substance. Anything that will alter the way I feel is acceptable, even if I already feel pretty good. In the last couple years, I've also taken a small shine to booze, prefer-ably the kind that tastes like something other than booze. For exam-ple, there's now a honey-flavored whiskey that I enjoy because it's like butterscotch that gets you drunk.

I've tried any number of things, pharmaceutical and otherwise, including running and writing this book. None of it works, at least not all the way. But I don't mind. If anything, I've learned to accept most of the bad shit with as much of a shrug as I can muster, because I have so much to be grateful for. Gratitude is the best antidote to pain I have found for every problem, except for slow Internet, which is the worst thing that can befall a human.

Mom manages her own pain with more grace than I would think possible. For all that she has lost, she retains a bright sense of humor. Yes, she has her bad days, but those are far outweighed by the good. Despite being largely confined to her condo, she remains interested in the world outside her window. To keep herself occupied during her days alone, she's dabbled in watercolors ("Terrible," she says) and photography ("I have no eye for it") and lately, she has begun asking me for advice on writing, a pastime she returns to now and again, and about which I have very little constructive advice to offer, especially considering that the book you are now reading is currently a year past its deadline. She makes friends easily: with her doctors, the woman who visits with her from the synagogue, the paramedics who right her when she falls and cannot stand back up. People like her. I like her. And, of course, I worry about losing her.

CHAPTER FOURTEEN

Fine, I will save a stupid human life!

I tried to save somebody's life once. I didn't know her personally, and if I ever knew her name, I have long since forgotten it. All I knew was that, like me, she was a student at NYU but, unlike me, she needed a bone marrow transplant. The girl had a rare bone marrow type, and they needed to cast as wide a net as possible to find her a match. Volunteers had fanned out across the campus, taping flyers to dormitory bulletin boards, begging students to register with the bone marrow people. I signed up, endured a small bloodletting, and walked away feeling like a hero. Obviously, I would not be a match, but I held my head high knowing I had done everything in my power to save that poor, dying girl. "I am an amazing human being," I thought to myself. There is no feeling quite so delicious as that of being virtuous without having had to do anything.

So it was with some alarm that I found myself, a couple of weeks later, in my dorm room speaking on the phone with the bone marrow people about the opportunity to save a life. As suspected, I was not a match for the NYU girl. But it turned out I *was* a potential match for a sickly, middle-aged man somewhere else in the country. Would I like to come in for further testing?

What kind of bullshit bait and switch was this? I'd signed on to save a fellow student, not some random dude. I had no idea that when I enrolled, the bone marrow people would then check my blood for *all* potential matches. I mean, there must be thousands of people—tens of thousands, perhaps—in need of bone marrow. Now they expected me to be some kind of bone marrow Oskar Schindler?

I hemmed and hawed with the guy. What did further testing involve? More blood tests, he told me. And if those tests matched? A small operation. An operation? Yes. How small an operation? Small. No, it wouldn't cost me anything. Would I like to come in? Well . . . "Because if you don't," he said, "it will be exactly the same as killing somebody."

(He didn't say that, but he might as well have.)

Ugh. Fine! FINE, I WILL SAVE A STUPID HUMAN LIFE! I made an appointment at the local hospital for further blood work. When I arrived, the receptionist directed me to the blood lab, located in a windowless tomb miles belowground. There, the technician directed me to a reclining pleather chair and instructed me to "just relax," as she drew out all of my blood. All of it. She took vial after vial after vial while I stared at a poster warning about sharing needles and communicable diseases. Damn it, I hadn't checked to see if the needle jutting into my arm looked secondhand or not. "Just one more," she said, wringing out my veins for any stray platelets she might have missed. Afterward she gave me a cookie, a thimble of orange juice, and a pamphlet about donating bone marrow.

I read the pamphlet on the subway ride home. It informed me that donating bone marrow requires surgery because bone marrow, unsurprisingly, is inside the actual bones. They have to drill down for it, like oil. Surgery requires hospitalization and anesthesia and recovery time and pain. How much pain? Minor, the pamphlet said. Some "bruising and soreness." How much is "some"? The pamphlet did not elaborate.

This was all pre-Internet, so I had no way of consulting Yelp for actual reviews of the procedure, but I have since done research and what I read seemed at odds with the "minor" pain promised in the pamphlet. One guy donated bone marrow without anesthesia and said, "It is the worst pain I have ever felt in my life." Yeah, dummy, because they frack your bones. Somebody else said, "The only things that are supposed to be more painful are a spinal tap and giving birth." So yes, it's minor pain when compared to being drawn and quartered.

Back in my dorm room, I struggled with my potential decision: Would I really go through actual surgery for a stranger? Actual *painful* surgery? All surgery entails a risk, however small, of death. Would I really risk my life? I tried to reason my way out of it. Maybe the guy was a dick. Maybe the guy was a pedophile. I mean, it made sense. Who other than a pedophile would put me out like this? Even as I asked myself these questions, I knew it didn't matter. If I matched, I would have the operation.

I didn't match.

Relief followed, but also an unexpected sadness. Without even realizing it, I'd geared myself up to be cut open, my marrow sucked through a silly straw. As crazy as it sounds, I'd almost begun looking forward to it. Surely we are meant to help others. That's the credo of every religion. Some of those religions even follow their own advice. And while I am not a person of faith, my own ethics demand that, when given the opportunity to help somebody else—even at some cost to myself—the right thing to do is to give that help. I sort of *wanted* to suffer for this stranger. A little bone drilling seemed an appropriate way to pay off whatever karmic debt I'd accrued. Plus, the pain pills would have been excellent.

I forgot about the man after that, but the episode awakened in me a desire to do helpful works. This would be a good thing had I actually followed through on that impulse. But I did not. Not then,

and not now. Yes, I contribute modest amounts to various charities throughout the year. And yes, I help my kids pick up litter on
Earth Day, but we get free ice cream at the end, so I'm not sure that
counts. I have lent my name to assorted causes and played poker
on television for hunger relief. But none of it costs me much in
any meaningful sense, and thus, none of it feels worthwhile. When
9/11 happened, the closest I got to being helpful was driving to the
local hospital to donate blood, only to be told they did not need any
more blood. I stopped at KFC on the way home, my reward for almost doing something good. I know I am supposed to help others as
surely as I know I am supposed to get that colonoscopy. And I will,
just not today.

Altruism produces some of the exact same results as running.
Both involve a certain amount of effort and anxiety. Both produce
feelings of healthfulness and well-being. Whenever I do either, I
vow to continue, only to disappoint myself with my lack of try-try-
again. Why are some people so much better than me? Why are some
people so goddamned good?

The bone marrow people did not forget about me. Even after
I moved multiple times and changed my name and faked my own
death, they somehow managed to find me twice more over the years.
Twice more they have contacted me as a potential match. Twice
more I have hauled myself to the nearest lab for additional blood
work. And twice more, I have felt that same anxiety build in my gut
for a week or so, only to be told that I am no longer a candidate for
donation. Each time I am pinged with that same combination of
relief and regret.

Volunteering to save that girl's life opened a Pandora's box on
my own humanity. Before that, it was easy enough to pretend that I
would remain forever untouched by other people's problems. After
all, I dealt with my own troubles without any outside assistance, and
aside from crippling depression, spiritual malaise, and emotional re-

tardation, I was fine. Shouldn't other people handle their problems the same way? Isn't self-reliance what America is all about? But when confronted with the opportunity to endure personal suffering for the sake of a stranger, something opened in my heart that I could no longer stuff back in. Out fluttered empathy and guilt and remorse and, worst of all, the desire to do better.

Thankfully, I got myself some Lexapro to make all those feelings go away. As the years have gone by, I have tried to do some good. I do all the correct little things: opening doors for people, giving up my subway seat for pregnant ladies and old people and old, pregnant ladies. When the Boy Scouts come to my door every year selling Christmas wreaths, I always buy one even though—and this is the crucial point—*I do not want a Christmas wreath*. But none of it taxes me very much. Better if I made myself a regular presence at the food pantry or the animal shelter or volunteered my time at a school. Better if I did better. But I don't.

CHAPTER FIFTEEN

"What happened to your face?"

I got punched in the face once. Maybe that doesn't seem like such a big deal. After all, a simple right hook to the jaw is nothing compared to the varied and wondrous mayhems conjured for us every day in our television shows, movies, and video games, where a single punch is nothing more than an appetizer to the *actual* violence about to occur. It is a prelude, an *amuse-bouche.* In my experience, though, being struck by the full force of another man's fist feels less like an appetizer and more like a Cheesecake Factory–size entrée of pain.

It happened during one of those few times in my life when I tried to be a Good Samaritan, a couple of years after I volunteered to save that girl's life with my stupid bone marrow. This was back in the bad old days of Times Square, before the successive mayoralties of His Honors Giuliani and Bloomberg scrubbed away the area's graffiti and grime, replacing the neighborhood peep shows with a Ripley's Believe It or Not. What had been the native habitat of grifters and skeevy streetwalkers gave way to an invasive species of sandal-wearing tourists spouting corny European accents. Many New Yorkers bemoaned the changes. They said New York had lost its edge, that it had become "Disneyfied." That may be true. But I suspect most of the people complaining didn't have to navigate those streets every morning, as I once did on my way to class, dodging crack peddlers and scabby hookers. It was a filthy, scary place and I do not mourn its passing.

Of the now-extinct species in Times Square, the only one I remember with a certain fondness is the three-card-monte hustler. Three-card monte is an ancient scam, dating back to at least the fifteenth century. The game is simple and probably familiar to most people. A hustler shuffles three cards, usually two red and one black, facedown on a flat surface. After several quick shuffles, a player wagers he can find the one black card of the three. The game looks easy enough: Any sufficiently attentive human can follow the black card as it weaves its way among its brothers. An unsuspecting mark is, therefore, surprised to discover players around him consistently guessing wrong, while he, the silent observer, always guesses right. Does he possess some preternatural card-following abilities? He must. What other explanation could there be? After watching several rounds, the mark steps forward to accept the dealer's offer to play. He confidently takes out his money, watches the shuffle, picks his card, and is stunned to discover that he has inexplicably chosen wrong, losing his money. Either he plays (and loses) again, or he stumbles away, feeling like a total fool, never realizing that the other players were all confederates in the con, all of them enacting an elaborate charade to entice suckers like himself into surrendering his dignity twenty dollars at a time.

I used to stop whatever I was doing to watch these games, reasoning it to be a relatively harmless scam. Players rarely lost more than twenty or forty dollars, and it was great entertainment watching the con unfold, time after time.

One afternoon, I took my normal station alongside a game. Beside me stood a Japanese tourist watching the game, riveted, slowly convincing himself he could beat it. Finally, as the dealer went back into his rap: "Twenty gets you forty, twenty gets you forty," I saw the guy reach into his pocket for cash. He stood there for a second, eyes intent on the game, a twenty-dollar bill in hand, deciding whether or not to play. The dealer finished his shuffle, and pointed to the guy: "Pick a card."

The tourist, perhaps sensing a losing proposition, wisely changed his mind and attempted to return the money to his wallet. The dealer wouldn't have it. "No, man! You took out your money. You got to pick a card!"

The Japanese tourist shook his head no, a nervous smile blooming on his lips.

"Pick a card!"

The tourist was confused, his English nonexistent. He tried to wave the guy off, tried to tell him he did not want to play. The dealer's accomplices, of which there were suddenly many, closed in around him, yelling, "You got to pick a card. You took out your money, you got to pick a card!"

The tourist seemed frightened, as anybody would be after finding themselves boxed in by a cluster of people jabbering at him in a foreign tongue. None of the other onlookers said anything, so I took it upon myself to act as the tourist's proxy. I did this because I am stupid. Stepping forward, I wedged myself between the tourist and the dealer and proffered my best legal argument: "C'mon man, leave him alone." (I used the word *man* to connote familiarity with the hustler's street patois and demonstrate my own hipness, and as a subtle means of letting him know I had once read *The Autobiography of Malcolm X*.)

After I spoke, all action froze. Blithely, I continued. "He shouldn't have to pick a card until he hands over the money." The defense rests. The defense is about to get punched in the face.

One of the lookouts issued a sharp, loud whistle. The dealer knocked over the stacked cardboard boxes he'd been using as his playing surface, spun on his heel, and strutted away. The crowd around him scattered like pigeons, along with the Japanese tourist I had just defended. Within seconds, it was like the game had never been there at all. Then, a guy about my height but beefier stepped up to me and, without a word, hit me as hard as he could square on the jaw.

BAM!

If you've never been punched in the face, here's how it feels: bad. It feels like getting slammed in the nuts, only the nuts are your face. Even so, I did not go down, a fact of which I remain ridiculously proud to this day. No, I remained standing. I stood and took the punch like a big, gaping idiot. Even now, twenty-plus years later, I can still recall the seismic force of that punch. Having never been punched in the face before, I have no way to compare its quality to other punches, but had I been a ringside announcer, I would have yelled something like, "Oh! Black just took a SHOT to the jaw! How is he even still standing? I admire him very much!"

After my face snapped back into place, I found myself locking eyes with my assailant. It was a weird, intimate moment, lasting less than a second. I have no idea what he saw in my eyes. Probably utter shock. But in his eyes—and I apologize in advance for what I'm about to say because it's going to make me sound like even more of a caricature of a bleeding-heart liberal than I actually am—I saw something more complicated. He looked pained and guilty and suddenly very young; he looked like a kid who'd just been caught stealing money from his mom's purse. In that microsecond before he stomped away—and this is the part I'm *really* embarrassed to write because I feel like such a pansy for even saying this—I felt sorry for him.

My assailant followed his coworkers down the block, leaving me alone on the sidewalk, a fresh white pain bulldozing its way across my skull. I mean, I wasn't literally alone; there must have been dozens of people who witnessed what happened, but nobody did anything. Nobody even asked if I was okay. Nor did I expect them to. This was big, bad New York, where people more or less expected to be assaulted at any given moment. In hindsight, I'm just lucky nobody picked my pocket after I got slugged. I remained rooted to the site of my assault for a long moment, letting the wobble in my brain slow and stop, my hand holding my jaw to keep it from shattering to the ground. I found my bearings and started walking.

By the time I got home, I could not close my mouth. The bottom would not align with the top, giving me the slightly baffled look of somebody who just saw a goat wearing a sombrero. My girlfriend of the time asked me what happened, but I didn't give her a direct answer.

"I got hit," I mumbled from the still-functioning side of my mouth.

She wanted details but I didn't feel like giving them. What about the police, she asked. I just shook my head no. There was no point. What was I going to tell them? I got punched in the face by a guy who looked pretty much like every other guy? Besides, talking hurt too much and I felt ashamed. Why did I get involved? If the tourist was dumb enough to take out his money, he was dumb enough to get ripped off. This was New York, after all. Don't come if you don't want to get conned or mugged or stabbed.

My girlfriend gave me ice for the swelling. I planted myself on the couch for two weeks. That's how long it took for my face to return to normal. Two weeks of soft foods and ibuprofen and responding to the same unwanted question again and again. "What happened to your face?" is a question nobody ever wants to answer.

After that, the world no longer felt quite so benign. I knew that crummy things sometimes happened to good people, but they weren't supposed to happen to *me*. And if some guy could just punch me out of the blue when I was simply doing my bit for international diplomacy, it seemed to me that anything could happen whenever it damn well chose. For the first time in my life, I felt physically vulnerable, which sent me down a wormhole of self-pity. What kind of man could not defend himself? What if it had been my girlfriend being attacked? What could I have done? The answer, immediate and stark: nothing.

Not much is expected of men anymore. No longer are we the family's sole providers. No longer assumed to hold positions of leadership over women. We are barely necessary for procreation. But in times of danger, men are still expected to step forward, still expected to rush into the burning building, to stay aboard the sinking ship, to risk life and limb for those more vulnerable than ourselves. But if a man cannot help even himself, then what good is he at all?

Now that I have a wife and two kids, my entire function is to ensure their safety and well-being. But just as I felt powerless over my assailant, just as I could do nothing to save my father, just as I cannot now cure my mother, I know I am running a fool's errand with my own family. Yes, I can give them a roof and food and I can make sure they buckle themselves in when we go for a drive. I can do all the things parents are supposed to do to keep their families safe. But the world is a big place and my dominion over it limited.

So far, as parents, we've been lucky. Our only real scare occurred when Ruthie was two, and a persistent high fever sent her to the hospital, the result of an infection from a faulty bladder valve. She spent several days there, hooked up to IVs, my wife and I trading time at her side while the other tended to Elijah. The valve eventually corrected itself without surgery. Now she's happy and healthy and eleven years old. Lucky. In the town next to mine here in the wilds of Connecticut, a gunman opened fire at an elementary school, killing twenty-six people, twenty of whom were children. It was a school just like the ones my kids were attending, at that moment, less than a dozen miles away. An event like that strikes a community like a meteor, devastating and unknowably alien. So I know how lucky we've been.

It is true that, ultimately, a punch to the face isn't that big a deal. My body, scrawny as it was, took the hit without suffering any lasting consequences. In the years that followed, I did nothing to better my chances in any such future encounters. I took no martial arts classes. I learned no kickboxing. No guns found themselves tucked into my underwear waistband. Maybe I kept my head down a little more. Maybe I grew a little more aware of my surroundings. Maybe I became a touch more cynical about my fellow man, and maybe if I stumbled upon a three-card-monte game again, I wouldn't put myself at risk to protect some stupid tourist. But, then again, maybe I would.

CHAPTER SIXTEEN

Douche nozzle

It's one thing to find yourself an unassuming victim of violence, still another to consciously put yourself in a position where violence is apt to be forced upon you. I did such a thing once. I shouldn't have.

On the occasion of the release of my first book, *My Custom Van (and 50 Other Mind-Blowing Essays That Will Blow Your Mind All Over Your Face)*, I found myself keeping careful tabs on my book's climb up the Amazon humor charts. To my surprise, the book seemed to be selling pretty well, rising all the way to number three, behind one of David Sedaris's perpetual bestsellers and *I Hope They Serve Beer in Hell*, by Tucker Max.

Considering I hadn't expected anybody to buy the book, the fact that it now seemed poised to, perhaps, become the number one best-selling humor book in the nation lit a fire under my ass, prompting me to do what I could to juice the numbers. Nothing sells better than controversy, so I used a blog I kept at the time to attempt to instigate a literary feud with my fellow authors, figuring I could maybe generate some attention, and, thus, book sales.

My first target was the guy immediately ahead of me on the charts, David Sedaris. I don't know David, and certainly had nothing against him, but I figured if he had a sense of humor, he might play along, which could be good for both of us. Obviously, I had no way of knowing if he would even hear of my "feud" with him, but I reasoned that the Internet is a big place, and somebody might draw his attention to it.

I decided to create a contest called "The First-Ever Turn David Sedaris into a Supervillain" competition, in which readers were invited to send in ideas for a David Sedaris supervillain. The winning entry was "Frenchy McStink," a Photoshopped image of David Sedaris's head grafted onto a Pepe LePew–looking cartoon skunk. The description of his supervillain powers read as such: "He draws in his victims with his nonchalant attitude and basket of well-arranged flowers. He then emits compelling and rather stinky excerpts from his latest collection of essays."

Silly, harmless fun, no? I wrote several blog posts excoriating Mr. Sedaris but never received a response. Although he didn't take my bait, I am told that once he was doing a book reading, and during the question-and-answer session somebody asked about his literary feud with Michael Ian Black. His response: "Who?"

Who indeed, Mr. Sedaris? Who indeed.

This feud proved so successful that my book actually passed Sedaris's on the humor charts, kicking me up to number two. I had never ranked so highly at anything in my life. I felt elated, invincible. Only Tucker Max remained ahead of me in my quest for the top spot. For those unfamiliar with Mr. Max's oeuvre, I present his self-description, taken from the back of his book:

"My name is Tucker Max, and I am an asshole. I get excessively drunk at inappropriate times, disregard social norms, indulge every whim, ignore the consequences of my actions, mock idiots and posers, sleep with more women than is safe or reasonable, and just generally act like a raging dickhead."

Tucker's book is a collection of stories detailing his drunken carousing and sexual misadventures with equally plastered girls, whereafter one or both of them invariably concludes the encounter with some variety of excrement and/or vomit. Naturally, the book was a huge, runaway bestseller, number one in the humor category for at least a year before I entered the charts. I could certainly understand the book's success: It's hard not to like a guy who so consistently throws up. Literature has a long list of lovable alcoholic scamps who act like pigs. The kid who wrote that book about heaven being real, for example.

So I set my targets on the humor category's white whale, Tucker Max. Like Sedaris, he would either never learn of our feud, or treat it like the idiocy I intended it to be. After all, if anybody knows idiocy, surely it is Tucker Max. The question: How to take him on? I'd already exhausted the literary feud idea, so I figured I needed to up the stakes. I would graduate to an actual feud. I would challenge Tucker Max to a fistfight.

In the open letter to him I published on my blog, I acknowledged that I could probably not beat him up because I could not beat up anybody, but said I had certain advantages over him that could possibly be exploited, chief among them the distinct possibility that he would show up to the fight drunk or hungover, and that he likely had cirrhosis of the liver, which might explode if I hit him there. I concluded by stating:

"So Tucker Max, you drunk, misogynistic motherfucker—I am calling you OUT! I am going to fist fuck every hole in your boozy little body until you crawl away like the sniveling little bitch that you are. YOU'RE DEAD!"

Please understand that, in my mind, this passed as clever. I figured it was so over-the-top that nobody could possibly take it seriously. If Tucker even saw the posting, he would laugh and respond with some sort of good-natured taunting on his part, which we could escalate into a hilarious running account of all the ways we planned on flaying the other. Within an hour of posting my blog, I had a reply from Tucker Max that read, simply, "I accept." He didn't seem to be laughing.

Oh, shit.

"I accept"? I tried to read between the lines for the "wink-wink, this is all in good fun" subtext, but there weren't many lines to read between and, finding none, I panicked. What was I supposed to do now? What did he actually mean, "I accept"? He couldn't possibly want to fight me. People don't *actually* fight, do they?

As I thought about it, I realized, yes, some people *do* actually fight, particularly people like Tucker Max, which is to say, people who have been insulted and then publicly challenged to a fistfight for no reason whatsoever.

I had to think long and hard about how to handle this. Maybe he didn't understand that I'd been kidding in my original post. I thought it'd been obvious, but I could possibly see how "I'm going to fist fuck every hole in your boozy little body" could be misconstrued as a serious declaration of intent. What other explanation could there be? So, to make it evident that I had no real intention of fighting him or anybody else, I decided to clarify my position to Tucker in a follow-up post, in which I would make it abundantly clear that I'd been having a laugh. I would do this by replying in such an outrageous manner that it would be obvious to one and all that the whole thing was just a silly put-on on my part—ha, ha, no hard feelings—and let's pretend it never happened. Here's what I wrote:

"So Tucker Max has officially accepted my challenge to a fight. Good. That was the easy part. The hard part? Deciding exactly how I am going to rearrange his face. Will I pluck out an eye and stuff it up his nostril? Will I make him choke down his own tongue until he throws it up and then sit on his head and force him to lap up his own puke like a bad little puppy? Or will I simply knock out his teeth and then use them as Chinese death stars that I throw into his black heart? I just do not know. But I do know this: Tucker Max is going down. How do I know? Because Tucker may have the athleticism, the muscles, the fighting skills, the experience, the guts, and the heart. But I have something he will NEVER have—I'm not sure what that is, but if I think about it long enough I will probably come up with something."

In retrospect, threatening to make somebody "choke down his own tongue" might not have been the best way to smooth the waters, because Tucker again wrote back, again without any humor, again saying he would be happy to fight me anytime, anywhere. For a humor writer, he didn't seem to have a very good sense of humor. On the other hand, his responses were, at least, concise.

Then, his fans started writing hateful and scary things. A fairly typical one follows:

> dude. you are a fucking idiot. yeah you're on basic cable . . . but it's VH1. I'd rather watch dead people decay than watch your stupid sorry ass on what you call "basic cable." Tucker Max is going to drop kick the teeth out of your mouth, dumbass. and after this fight is over, and you're frantically trying to hold together whatever manhood you have left (which I doubt you have much to start with) EVERYONE is going to be laughing at your pathetic excuse of a human being. have fun being the laughingstock of the century.

I didn't want everyone laughing at my pathetic excuse of a human being. I didn't want that at all, but what was I going to do? This situation had all the classic hallmarks of being a major oopsy on my part. Somehow, I had accidentally/deliberately put myself in the untenable position of challenging a frat-house jock to a fistfight. How could I have been so stupid? How could I extricate myself from this predicament with grace? I couldn't. Either I would have to fight Tucker Max or be known forevermore throughout the land as a coward.

Aha! I had found my way out! I would be known as a coward!

The more I thought about it, the more sense it made. First of all, I *am* a coward. There's no shame in being a coward, if being a coward is defined as somebody who is afraid to get into a fistfight he cannot win. For example, I wouldn't be afraid to fight a three-year-old, because I know I could win that fight. In a fight with a three-year-old, I would be the brave one and the kid would be the coward. Cowardice is, perhaps, just another word for knowing your chances. Besides, what consequences would I face for my cowardice? None. I wasn't at war; I wasn't in danger of being shot at dawn for fleeing the battle. The only bullets I would take would be from online commenters. Those are bullets I could handle. I mean, c'mon—I'm a married father of two. Guys like me don't fight. At worst, we litigate.

Once I accepted my own cowardice, the solution fell into place. When asked, and I was frequently asked in those days, I would tell people the truth: I could not possibly fight Tucker Max for the simple reason that, if I were to fight him, he would beat me up. People seemed pretty disappointed with this response, because they wanted to see blood. People are awful in that way. Not that I blame them. Were it not my blood we were discussing, I would have wanted to see the same.

My book climbed no higher on the humor charts, even though I set off on a nationwide book tour to promote the thing. As part of my tour, I did a series of radio interviews. One of them was with a station in San Diego who told me they had a surprise for me. "Great," I said, "I like surprises." The DJs then put Tucker Max on the line, who had graciously stepped off the set of the movie adaptation of his book to threaten to beat me into unconsciousness. Tucker was soft-spoken and businesslike, telling me he couldn't wait to hit me. He didn't want to hurt me, he said, just knock me out, which I thought was very gracious. He was so anxious to do this, he said, he would do whatever it took to make it happen, even offering to "walk from

Louisiana to San Diego" if that was what it took to get the fight done. I tried to play it all off as the joke I had intended it to be, but Mr. Max would not cooperate.

Afterward, he e-mailed me, saying he would "help me find a graceful way out of this," which actually made me feel worse about myself than refusing to fight him. I told him that, while I appreciated his offer, I would extricate myself in my own way, meaning I would confess my cowardice and allow the haters to, as my ex-girlfriend Taylor Swift says, hate hate hate.

It took several months for all the hate mail to stop flowing into my inbox, and even now, once in a while, somebody will remind me that I once threatened to beat up Tucker Max and did the fight ever happen and why not and oh, I see, you're chickenshit and have no pride in yourself, which usually ends the conversation with a series of embarrassed shrugs and sighs on both of our parts because there is no shame for a man quite like cowardice.

Now that I have put some years between myself and that brief but embarrassing episode, I have to ask myself if I would have done anything differently given the chance. Yes, I definitely learned a couple lessons. First and foremost, don't challenge anybody to a fistfight who might actually accept. This is an important rule for authors and people in general. Second, if you do challenge somebody to a fight, have an exit plan—either fight the fight or have some sort of clever stratagem to get out of it. Contract malaria, for example, which has the dual advantages of being debilitating and highly contagious. Nobody is going to fight you if you have malaria. Finally, when engaging in a feud of any sort, only do so in a way that ensures you have the upper hand. The moral high ground, for example, is a great place upon which to stand. Or, if you are going to take the low road, you must do so in a way that incapacitates your opponent. I took neither road, and that made all the difference.

If anybody knows Tucker Max, please tell him I am sorry. I was wrong to call him out in a public forum, particularly since he had done nothing more to earn my ire than be successful. Furthermore, I had no business challenging him to fisticuffs if I did not intend to follow through. I was wrong to do that and I am sorry. The simple fact of the matter is, I am a coward when it comes to Tucker Max, and I deeply regret using a crass marketing stunt to sell books. That kind of talk has no place between authors of our caliber, and I deeply regret my actions. On the other hand, if anybody knows David Sedaris, please tell him I will kick his Francophile ass from here to kingdom come. That little fucker has it coming.

CHAPTER SEVENTEEN

Dog and pony show

I am going deaf. That is not some bit of comic exaggeration on my part. I have been to the audiologist, had my ears peered into with the ear-peering machine, taken that test where you raise your left and right hands when you hear the left and right beeps (or in my case, don't hear the left and right beeps), and the results were definitive: My hearing is bad, likely to get worse, and I know why.

The story of my hearing loss begins with my contempt for high school. I hated it. Everybody hated high school, and if you didn't, then you shouldn't be reading this book, because this book is for cool people. High school had all the mind-numbing tedium of the worst office job in the world combined with all the potential for imminent, grievous bodily harm that exists in your finer state penitentiaries. For my four years, I did what I could to endure. This meant keeping my head down, cultivating a small group of (mostly) female friends, and trying to stay out of the crosshairs of the roving bands of feral jocks that roamed the school's hallways.

During my junior year, a few of us started getting into punk rock, natural musical sanctuary for the righteous and unloved. My musical evolution from Wham! to the Dead Kennedys took about six months, a time when I haunted local record shops for bands with the freakiest names I could find in the hopes of discovering the aggressive hardcore punk I'd grown to love. Sometimes this worked, and sometimes I came home with a 10,000 Maniacs album. It wasn't like today, when you can just Google "punk rock" and get a billion hits. Back then, there was no definitive source for these underground sounds. The only place to hear it was the local college radio station, WPRB, whose faint signal I could pick up if I held my radio antenna between my thumb and pointer finger while standing on my dresser. Late at night, they played an intimidating blend of scary-sounding bands like Black Flag, the Circle Jerks, and the Day-Glo Abortions. Did I like the music? Not really. In my secret heart, I still preferred Duran Duran, but I liked punk's energy and menacing vibe. I liked their countercultural stance. In a time when Bon Jovi ruled the world, a little counterculture seemed like a very good thing, indeed. After a year or so of listening to this stuff, the thought occurred: Surely I could make music at least as terrible as this.

My friend Tim and I decided to start our own punk band. Starting a band in high school is a simple and straightforward proposition because the options for personnel are so few. Tim played bass, so we had that covered. Some guy we kind of knew named Jeff played guitar, so we asked him to join the band, and somebody told us that Mark, the weird metalhead with the long hair and the copy of *The Anarchist Cookbook*, played drums, so we invited him, too. I didn't play anything so I would sing. Or, rather, "sing."

That night, I remember telling Mom I was starting a punk band.

"You didn't ask me if you could start a punk band," she said. I explained to her that asking permission from one's mother to join a punk band kind of defeated the whole point.

The first order of business for any band is to come up with a name. Should it be aggressive, like Black Flag? Jokey, like the Circle Jerks? Confrontational, like MDC, which stood either for Millions of Dead Cops or Millions of Dead Christians? We went for ironic and named our band "the Pleased." Do you get it? Do you get the irony? Because we *weren't* pleased. We were anything *but* pleased. We were PISSED OFF. At who? (I know it's "whom," but punk rockers don't use that word.) You guessed it, motherfucker: society.

We took the Pleased more seriously than anything else in our lives, practicing every day at Mark the drummer's house. He had his kit set up in the family dining room; it would have looked out of place in an ordinary home, but Mark's mother was a stay-at-home hoarder, so it fit right in among the piles of clothing, plastic housewares, and unopened Christmas presents from the previous year. If anything, Mark's drum area was probably a little *more* organized than the rest of the house.

We'd play for a couple hours most days after school, bashing out covers of simple songs, and afterward, I'd notice my ears ringing for a few minutes. Never too long and never too bad. Just like somebody was fiddling around in my ears with a Q-tip attached to a cowbell. It would fade after a little while and I would go about the rest of my day.

Our first show was a battle of the bands at a nearby school, which we fucking won, using the prize money to buy ourselves a proper microphone. Then our own high school had a Winter Party and we played that, and we fucking kicked ass. Afterward, they had to bring in special equipment to clean up all the panties tossed at us.

Because we were punk rock in a period when punk rock had mostly fallen off the map, we didn't really know how to look. This is post–Sex Pistols, pre-Nirvana, so the closest role model we could find was Duckie from *Pretty in Pink*, who in retrospect seems less like a punk rocker and more like an adolescent struggling with his sexuality. But he dressed weird, and that was good enough for us.

The deeper we got into the band, the more apparent certain shortcomings became. First and foremost was the fact that Tim didn't really know how to play bass. Of all of us, Tim looked the most like a punk rocker. Beefy and occasionally Mohawked, Tim rode a skateboard and scowled a lot. He seemed to live and breathe a kind of rough punk ethos: a real live-fast, die-young kind of guy despite the fact that he lived in a comfortable suburban home with his parents, who raised championship shih tzus. What Tim didn't do was practice the bass. He could kind of pluck his way through our songs, but his main musical skill was looking cool onstage. For a punk band, this is a not unimportant talent. After all, what did Sid Vicious contribute to the Sex Pistols other than looking cool and stabbing his girlfriend? Not much. It was Tim the girls swooned over, so much so that, the morning after one of our shows, a girl I had a crush on told me she had just seen Tim's band play. "Have you ever seen them?" she asked me.

After a while, we began writing our own material. The first lesson in any writing is, of course, "Write what you know." I definitely took this to heart when I wrote my first song, "The Race," about racial politics in apartheid-era South Africa. Obviously, nobody understood that subject better than me.

Once we had enough songs, we decided to record an album. This is back in the days when you couldn't just push a button on your phone and pop out a radio-ready MP3. You had to actually go to a recording studio and lay out actual money. Lots of money. We found a local studio that could do the job for five thousand dollars, a sum that would have been unobtainable were it not for the fact that Mark's father was in the construction business. In New Jersey, "construction business" means mobbed up. Which meant it wasn't any big thing for Mark to steal five grand in cash from his father's sock drawer.

Once we had our record (actually cassette), we began hawking it to our classmates and blindly sending it to record labels in the hopes that one of them was looking for a teenage punk band with a bass player who couldn't play bass and a singer who couldn't sing.

Although we didn't get any interest from labels, our ambitions grew. Maybe we could really be something. We started playing a few local club shows. Then somebody noticed an ad in a local alternative weekly. CBGB, the venerable punk institution, was hosting "audition nights" every Monday. We called. Could we audition? Yes, we could.

"Okay. I got you down in three weeks," the guy on the other end told us. "The more people you bring the more likely you are to pass the audition."

Well, that makes sense. If we bring more people, they are more likely to cheer for us, management is more likely to be impressed, and we are more likely to pass the audition. Good tip, guy on other end of the phone.

Holy shit, we were going to play CB's! Things just got real. If we were going to audition for CB's, that was an audition we were going to pass. Our practice sessions took on a new intensity, and so did the ringing in my ears. Now, I would find myself unable to hear much for an hour or two after a rehearsal or show. Everything would sound muffled and distant, but I didn't say anything about it to anybody. Plus, I was also blowing out my voice each day, so I had to deal with that, too. Between the two things—ears and voice—the voice seemed like the more urgent matter, since I couldn't perform if I couldn't sing. I suppose I wouldn't have been able to perform if I'd gone deaf, either, but that thought never occurred to me. Nor did it occur to me to wear earplugs. Earplugs weren't punk rock.

The day of the CBGB show, we caravanned to New York with every single Pleased fan we could muster, which totaled about five. We pulled up to the club and unloaded our gear and inhaled for the first time that sour CB's air: a potent brew of dank beer and BO. Record deal or no, walking into that club made me feel like we'd made it. Was there ever a more perfect time to unleash the full fury of our punk rock dystopian sonic nightmare than four-thirty on a Monday afternoon? Hell, no.

We played our show fast and tight. Fifteen minutes, six songs. Afterward, I pried a tiny black splinter from the stage and shoved it into my pocket, a souvenir. My ears rang all the way back to New Jersey.

Did we pass the audition? A few days went by without any word from CB's. Then a week. Then two. Finally, one day at rehearsal, I summoned the nerve to call the club myself. "CB's," said the voice on the other end.

"Yeah, hi. Uh, my name is Michael. My band the Pleased played the audition night a couple weeks ago and we were wondering if we passed."

A long pause.

"Yeah, you passed."

"Seriously?"

"Yeah." Another pause. "Congratulations."

Holy shit, we passed! I hung up and told the other guys. We couldn't believe it. We danced around the room, cheering ourselves. Passing that audition felt like punk validation; it was like getting a French kiss from Joey Ramone himself. So what exactly did passing the audition mean? Until that moment, I never thought to ask. If pressed, I would have assumed it meant we would soon be regularly playing CB's, opening for our musical heroes. Further, it would probably mean a lot of travel, since we'd soon start touring, plus we'd have to find somebody to take on the road with us to drive the van and deal with all the merch. Or maybe we should just get a tour bus to save on hotel expenses. Dealing with all the logistics would be a nightmare, so we should maybe think about hiring a tour manager, but how much would that cost? Then we would be having to decide whether to sign with the majors or stick with an indie label. Did we want to play *SNL* or would that look like selling out? Wow, passing this audition was definitely cool, but I could see that our impending success was going to present a host of problems we hadn't anticipated. Not that I was complaining; I'd signed up for this rocket ride. Now it was time to shoot the moon.

We never heard from CBGB again.

Never did it occur to me—or to the other guys—that Monday afternoons and evenings are probably a pretty slow time in the world of live music venues and that one way to bring in a little business would be to hold "auditions," and to ask the bands gullible enough to sign up to bring as many fans as they could—fans who would have to pay a five-dollar cover and purchase a two-drink minimum. Never did it occur to us that the audition was a scam. After all, punk rockers don't scam other people. That went against the whole punk rock credo, at least as interpreted by four New Jersey teenagers. We were honest and true, a small force for good in a sick and corrupted world. It never occurred to us that the whole thing was just a dog and pony show. It never occurred to us at all.

We graduated not long after that. Three of us would be headed off to college in the fall, and Mark would continue his career stealing credit card information. The band would not survive, could not survive—and yet, we had passed that audition, hadn't we? Maybe some hope still existed for us. Maybe we could each take a year off from college and petty thievery to give this thing a real go.

But if we were going to give the Pleased a shot, we had to do something about Tim. The simple fact of the matter was that Tim could not play bass, at least not to the level expected of a band that had passed the audition at CBGB. After much back-and-forth, we decided Tim had to go.

Tim, who had cofounded the band. Tim, the only legitimate punk among us. Tim, who was my best friend in the group and who loved the band more than even I, who loved the band with every fiber of my being.

We called a rehearsal at Mark's house and I delivered the news. He took it with grace, which is to say he screamed, "Fuck you guys!"

and stormed out of the house calling us assholes and traitors as he went.

Which we were.

Which I was.

To this day, firing Tim from the Pleased is one of my life's biggest regrets. Had I stopped to soberly consider the situation even for a minute, I would have realized we were done. Were any of us really going to give up college to play shitty dive bars with what basically amounted to a below-average punk rock cover band? Of course not. Why couldn't I just leave well enough alone, and let the Pleased die a noble, punk rock death? Did I really believe my singing was any better than Tim's bass playing? We were equally inept, and yet I somehow convinced myself that he was the band's single liability, that without him, we'd have a record deal and a shitty van and be driving across the country and crashing on couches and sleeping with groupies. Why did I blow up my friendship with Tim over a pipe dream? God, I was such an asshole.

Years went by. Somebody invented Facebook. One day, I got a friendship request from an old friend. Tim. Did I want to get together, have lunch, catch up?

We met in the city. He looked the same, only with a sleeve of tattoos he hadn't had before. He seemed mellow and happy and he asked me all about my life. I answered. When I finished, I asked about his. He'd gone to art school for a while, pissed around, done a little of this and that, started roadying for some bands, then put together a band of his own. He wasn't playing bass anymore. He was singing. Or "singing." They had a record deal. They toured the world in shitty vans, crashed on couches, and preached that good punk rock sermon to all the righteous and unloved teenagers of the world. It blew my mind. Tim, the seventeen-year-old punk rocker who I could not imagine doing anything else with his life, is now in his forties, and he is a professional punk rocker.

For its short existence, the Pleased meant everything to me. It meant validation. It meant belonging to something at a time when I didn't feel like I belonged anywhere. But now I am going deaf. The ringing in my ears doesn't stop, a low-grade tinnitus (pronounced TIN-i-tis, not tin-EYE-tis, as the audiologist told me) that will never get better and may end up degrading my hearing to the point that I need a hearing aid sooner rather than later. Many times, I find myself responding to people without having had any idea what they've just told me, nodding or laughing as I deem appropriate based on visual cues. The word I say with the most frequency is "what?" as in, "What did you just say?" It drives Martha crazy. It drives *me* crazy.

Was my year as a punk rocker worth losing my hearing over? New Jersey sucked. My home life sucked. School sucked. The band didn't suck. The band gave me the ability to endure everything else. When we played, I felt invulnerable. I felt electric. I felt the most like myself I had ever felt until that point. So was it worth it?

Hell, no.

No, I'd much rather have my hearing than those memories, especially considering the sour taste I still have in my mouth for how it ended. But since I can't get my hearing back, I'll take the memories. I'll take the rehearsals in Mark's hoarder house and the Battle of the Bands and the cassette and my six songs on the beat-up old stage in that old punk mecca, gone now, replaced by a John Varvatos clothing store that sells four-hundred-dollar pairs of shoes. Forming that band was the first time I'd undertaken a serious creative endeavor, the first time I thought, "I could do that," then actually done it. That's a valuable lesson for anybody. So even though the trade-off is that I now have to turn up the television volume to unacceptable levels when watching anything more narratively complicated than *Sesame Street*, I'll take it. It may not be a fair trade, but all things considered, I'm pleased.

CHAPTER EIGHTEEN

I need some reassurance that everything is going to be okay

People who say you should do things all the way or not do them at all have obviously never run a half marathon. Even its name says you will only be doing things in half measures, so it's a cop-out right off the bat. But half of something extremely hard and tedious is still something pretty hard and tedious.

A full marathon is 26.2 miles, the distance from New York City to Tokyo. Divide that by two and you've still got 13.1 miles, which is still a hell of a long way to go by foot. Could I run that far? I first asked myself that question toward the end of my sedentary winter following the 10K I'd run the previous autumn. I hadn't exercised at all during the cold months, preferring the company of warm cookies to that of the chilly woods, making all sorts of excuses to myself as to why I could not possibly run: The ground is too muddy, too cold, too wet, my complexion too delicate, my chakra misaligned, etc. But as winter melted into spring, some primal urge started poking at me. Didn't I need to get back out there? I mean, here I was, forty-two years old, lazing about, feeling like a fat squidge.

Could I really commit to a training regimen that would have me out there four days a week, running ever-increasing miles in anticipation of a thirteen-mile footrace? Of course I could. The half marathon was only a little more than twice as long as the 10K, which hadn't been terrible. Just do two of those plus a little more and boom, that's a half marathon. I could do that, just not all at once. Maybe spaced out over a couple weeks.

After a long time off from exercise, the hardest thing to do is taking that first step. Tying my running shoes felt like climbing a mountain. Ugh—was I really going to do this again? I did not want to. Did not want to. Did not want to. I repeated this mantra down the stairs from my bedroom and out the front door and onto my driveway, where I set my running app for three miles and began my first slow jog in months and I did not want to. But I did.

My new training program called for a lot of running, up to twelve miles a day toward the end. That is *so much* running, the kind of running where, when you take a shower afterward, your nipples hurt because they have chafed against the fabric of your technical shirt. If these shirts are so technical, why don't they have an anti-nipple-chafe feature? Bloody nipples are no joke. I mean, they're kind of a joke if they're happening to somebody else, because the idea of bloody nipples is at least a little bit funny. I'd heard about such a thing but never experienced it, and although it hurt, I have to say I felt proud that an athletic endeavor I undertook was so difficult it actually caused my nipples to bleed. That's pretty hard-core.

The toughest thing about training for the half marathon was the time commitment: hours per week, hours that could have been more fruitfully been spent not running. Why did I persist, week after week, through the summer heat and into the chilly days of autumn? What was my fascination with running? What was I looking for from the simple activity of placing one foot in front of the other faster than normal? What did I want? The truth is, I knew what I wanted from running, but I couldn't quite bring myself to admit it: I wanted enlightenment. And this is where are all my convoluted feelings about my body and Mom's declining health and aging and my own fear of death and praytheism congeal into a goopy sludge. This is the nexus. It is a stupid nexus, to be sure, but I could not quite shake the idea that running could save me.

It's not such a crazy idea. After all, lots of mundane activities give meaning to people's lives. Think of the ladies who volunteer to knit tiny pink and blue hospital caps for newborn babies. Or people who meditate. Or fish. Can't we find enlightenment in anything if we look hard enough? I don't think a profound spiritual awakening is too much to ask from jogging a few miles. It's what I'd been looking for from the moment I took my first step as a runner. It's a hard thing to admit because it seems so foolish, but it's the truth. I have no church. I have no faith. My mother is falling apart in pieces and my children are growing up and I am getting old and I need some reassurance that everything is going to be okay.

How could running possibly provide such reassurance? I did not know, but some part of me believed it would. If I just ran enough miles, suffered enough, climbed enough hills, put myself through a terrible enough physical crucible, I might emerge on the other side somehow (and this is the word that is most embarrassing but also the truest description of what I sought) holy.

I did what I could when I ran. I breathed and repeated nonsensical little mantras. I tried to clear my head of extraneous thoughts, to focus on one step following the other through space. I tried listening to music and not listening to music. When the highs came, they felt delicious but not revelatory, which only encouraged me to dig deeper, to dredge up more. I knew the highs were illusions, just endorphins flooding into my nervous system, but I thought if I sifted through them, I could find something richer, gold in the dirt of my earthy emotions. And when I suffered, I tried to cast the suffering in metaphysical terms, the price mystics paid for enlightenment. And when I let the hot water run over my head and sting my bloody nipples at the end of my workout, I tried to hold on to whatever I'd learned during my exertions. What had I learned?

Not much. Possibly nothing.

I didn't know if I would recognize what I sought if I ever found it. What was I even looking for? Would it be like *The Matrix*, when Keanu Reeves starts seeing binary code everywhere? Or would it be like that time I took LSD in the Badlands of South Dakota and saw the gates of hell open before me? If I had to put it into words, I would say I was seeking a spiritual orgasm. If I couldn't have that, I supposed I would settle for a traditional orgasm.

I got neither, which only strengthened my resolve. I began reading accounts of ultramarathons, those fifty- and hundred-mile races that have grown in popularity over the last few years. What else would propel people to run those distances other than the same quest I found myself on? We all sense that our limits extend farther than we know, and that, in pushing ourselves past what we believe possible, we find something new, something otherwise unseen. The question was: What do we find? None of the ultramarathoners I read about said anything about enlightenment. Instead they discussed blackened toenails and diarrhea cramps and sunburn in the morning and hypothermia at night. Pictures of them at the eighty- or ninety-mile mark showed gaunt and haggard zombies, eyes glazed, stumbling toward a finish line still miles in the distance. They looked more beat-up than beatific. Yet, most of them came back time and time again. Why?

I scrutinized my body for changes. Yes, enlightenment was one of my goals, but having a ripped, hot bod was another. Little progress on that front, either. Sure, I dropped a few pounds but I did not acquire Bruce Whitehall's lean physique and gleaming teeth. I still looked like me, a version of myself pretty much indistinguishable from the guy who'd been sitting on the couch all those months. So if I looked the same and felt the same, what the hell was I doing?

As my half-marathon day approached, I conspired with my mountain bike buddy Matt to run the thing together. Matt is a better athlete than me, and I worried that I wouldn't be able to keep up with him during the long slog. Not that it mattered much. The point was to run my own race regardless of how quickly Matt ran. If I fell behind, I fell behind. No big deal. I mean, I obviously wouldn't let myself fall *too far* behind. Or at all. Fuck it: I wasn't going to let Matt beat me. Also, I instructed my family where and when to meet, confident Martha would not screw it up this time. If she did, I would not only divorce her, I would start a letter-writing campaign to Amnesty International to have her declared a violator of human rights. She swore to me up and down that she and the kids would be waiting for me at the finish line.

So there we were, several hundred of us, gathered just beyond the starting line outside a middle school somewhere in the wilds of Connecticut. The racecourse would take us in a loop through a series of cutesy neighborhoods before dumping us onto Main Street for a triumphal processional to glory. When the starter pistol fired, we shuffled along with the herd to the starting line, and then onto the course itself, our numbers gradually spreading out until Matt and I found ourselves among no more than half a dozen runners at a time. We kept careful pace because I swore to myself not to make the same mistake I had in my first race, going out too fast and then faltering at the end. It was a good promise to make and an impossible one to keep. I ran much too fast because of the adrenaline, yes, but also because I'm a buffoon.

"How're you feeling?" Matt would ask me as we huffed along.

"Good, man!" Which was true for the first few miles. Less so for the next few, and not at all true as we approached the ten-mile mark. Matt began pulling away from me a little bit at a time. At first I tried to keep up, but I eventually concluded it was a fool's errand. I'd run too fast in an effort to stay with my buddy and now I was paying the price. At the ten-mile mark, it's tempting to exalt, "I've run ten miles! There's only three miles to go!" Which is true, except that, after running so many, each subsequent mile takes on a "dog's year" quality.

Finally I told Matt to go on without me, words I'd only expected to ever use after being pinned down in an ice crevasse following an avalanche. "You go ahead," I panted, knowing that, as a gentleman, he would refuse.

"Okay," he said, kicking into a gear that I not only didn't possess after ten miles of running, but had never possessed. After Matt disappeared over a distant hill, I began having insidious thoughts like: "Why don't you just take a little break? Nobody will know. You could just sit down for a few minutes and rest. C'mon, Michael, you've earned it. Just stop and get your shit together for a second. You don't want to finish this race looking less than handsome. Take a seat— that's not cheating."

And, of course, it's true: Resting isn't cheating. But it *felt* like cheating, and I did not want to cheat. And this is where I began to discover what all those miles of training had been good for. While seeking enlightenment, I discovered something else: fortitude. Truth be told, I would have preferred the enlightenment, but at mile ten, you take what you can get.

"No," I told myself. "I'm not going to stop. I might slow down, but I'm not going to stop. And I'm not going to walk."

I ran those last few miles feeling like I had somebody standing on my feet. All the while, my mind's little hobgoblin would not shut up: "Why run at all? What's the point? What's the point of anything when you really think about it, you know?" But once my mind started resorting to existential questions like "What's the point?" I knew I had it beat. Because even though I sought transcendence, part of me suspected there had been no point from the very beginning. The point was, in fact, beside the point. Finishing was the only point, and the only way to make the point was to finish.

Signs lined the course for the last mile: ½ MILE TO GO, ¼ MILE TO GO, 200 YARDS TO GO. Approaching the end, I straightened my posture and put on a burst of speed, which, in my case, meant going from jogging incredibly slowly to jogging slightly less incredibly slowly. Up ahead, I saw Martha and the kids. They'd made it! I practically flew (hobbled) across the finish line in two hours and seven minutes, which is only a bit less than mediocre. Somebody put a medal around my neck, and I circled back to my family, where I received hugs and congratulations and the expected "you smell" from my daughter. Then I sat down and put my head between my legs, because if I didn't, I was going to throw up.

Afterward, as I stood in the shower at home peeling protective Band-Aids from my nipples, I found myself wondering at my curious lack of elation. I'd done it, but having done it, I didn't experience any particular pride of accomplishment. Sure, finishing felt better than not finishing, but I'd expected something *more*. It felt like that same emptiness I'd had throughout my training, the feeling there was something out there, something just out of reach, something that could answer some question I didn't know how to ask.

Matt called a couple weeks later to ask if I wanted to sign up with him for the following year's New York City Marathon. I gave it some thought. I no longer doubted that I could do it. With enough time and training, I could run twenty-six point two miles. But after mulling it over, I turned him down. Running, for all its merits—merits that I could not then and cannot now identify by name—did not seem to be giving me that ephemeral something I'd been seeking. It provided no answers beyond that to the question: "Should I eat three bowls of Froot Loops before running?" (Answer: no.) Maybe I would keep running or maybe I wouldn't, but to subject myself to further months of training for the opportunity to run through the city's five boroughs didn't seem worth it, especially considering the fact that I usually do what I can to avoid traveling those boroughs even by car.

I still run. Not often. I keep meaning to get back into a routine with it, but somehow it doesn't happen. Probably because I don't want it to. But I still think about those ultramarathoners out there in the mountains somewhere, running through the night, their vision narrowed to wedges of headlamp light as they trudge through fifty, seventy-five, a hundred miles. I think about the physical and emotional vicissitudes they must endure, and some not insignificant part of me wants to be out there with them, to know what they know, to strip away every thought, to undo everything that I am until I am no more than a body moving through space. I think about them a lot and I wonder what they learn out there and I wonder if they are different when they return. And when I am done thinking about them, I take a nap, because fuck that.

CHAPTER NINETEEN

A bad seed

Mom describes her younger sister as a "real piece of work," which she does not mean as a compliment. Her name was Ilene. Although she sometimes called herself Susan. And sometimes Kelly.

Ilene/Susan/Kelly stumbled through trouble for the whole of her life, wheedling and lying her way into and out of jobs, homes, relationships. She had seven—SEVEN—husbands and, toward the end, several female lovers. While doing research for this book, I found a few mentions of her in newspapers, the only positive one being a brief notice of promotion, in 1985, to national sales manager for a company that sold two-way radios, antennas, and something called "battery conditioners." Three years later, there is a bankruptcy declaration in the amount of $130,000, followed several months after that by a sheriff's sale of her condominium in Oklahoma. Then nothing until 1997, when she was arrested in South Florida on two counts of assault and battery. A court date was set, but I don't believe the trial ever happened. In December of that year, she killed herself. She was fifty-one.

"I think she was born a bad seed," says Mom. I'm not sure I believe that children are born "bad," but it is certainly true that Ilene found trouble from an early age. Ilene ran with the bad crowd, listened to the bad music. Smoked the bad stuff. Did the bad things. Had there been a nearby Jewish motorcycle gang, she no doubt would have joined. Once, while Mom was helping her own mother move, she found some documents shoved into the back of a drawer. The papers mandated a court-ordered abortion for Ilene, who was twelve or thirteen at the time. Needless to say, Grandma and Ilene did not get along. "I guess it was like pure hatred. My mother really hated her. She would never admit that, but she did."

Ilene got engaged young, to a local boy, then jilted him for her first husband, a sailor who moved next door to live with his mother. She fell for the snappy naval uniform and the promise of adventure at far-flung naval bases. Within months of meeting, they married.

Their brief union produced a son, Shawn, born a few years before me. I have no photos of Shawn, and the only mental image I have of him comes from a pencil drawing Sailor Boy made that used to hang on Grandma's wall. It's a good drawing. It shows Grandpa, bald and heavy, seated on a living room chair, battleship tattoo visible on his forearm. He's jiggling a newborn on his knee, my brother Eric. Shawn, not yet three, stands to his side, looking up at Grandpa, a stuffed animal hanging from his hand. The drawing was made the same year Shawn died. He suffocated to death in a plastic bag at home.

Ilene and the sailor divorced. After a couple years, she married again. She and her new husband adopted a baby boy. I ask, but Mom doesn't know where the baby came from. "She might have handed five bucks to somebody in a parking lot for all I know," she says. For a short while the family seemed happy enough, but soon after the boy turned two, Ilene left, leaving the baby in his father's care. This would be a pattern throughout her life, a frenetic wanderlust that upended untold lives. The father raised the son and, understandably, cut off all contact with Ilene's side of the family. Mom says she has been trying to find her adopted nephew for years without success.

About ten years after that, while "on the lam from creditors," according to my mother, Ilene found herself in Oklahoma, where she met a cowboy. Their marriage, her fifth or sixth, produced another son. When the boy was still a toddler, she left them, too. The cowboy remarried, then abandoned his new wife, leaving his son in the care of a stepmother who seems to have been the first person in the boy's life who wanted and loved him.

Every once in a while, Ilene would drop back into her son's life, materializing from space to reconnect with him for a few days or weeks before disappearing again, sometimes for years. Then, when he was eleven or twelve, she somehow wrested custody of her son from the stepmother. Ilene took the boy down to Florida and tried to play mother. One day after school, he walked in on Ilene unconscious. She'd attempted suicide, leaving her body for her middle-school-age son to find. This was the first suicide attempt that I know of, but it would obviously not be the last.

The boy headed back north. He moved back in with his stepmother and, no surprise, began dabbling with drugs, which led to addiction, which led to him becoming unruly and violent. She kicked him out of the house and he drifted, sometimes homeless, to Los Angeles, where he cleaned himself up. That's where Martha and I met him. He'd been clean for a while, and he struck us both as such a lovely, friendly guy. We hung out with him a few times, but we haven't seen him since we moved back to the East Coast fifteen years ago. I spy on him from Facebook from time and time, though, and in the photos he posts he seems healthy and happy. He's married to a man who looks weirdly like him, and he seems to have regular employment and a good life. Thank God the trail of destruction his mother caused seems to have ended.

I only met Aunt Ilene the few times she visited New Jersey. All adults intimidated me when I was a kid, but I remember feeling a different kind of unease around Ilene. Wariness, maybe. There was something glamorous about her, in an Amy Winehouse sort of way. She looked a bit like my mom, but skinnier, with most of her weight seeming to come from her hair and lip gloss. In my mind's eye, she is forever peering down at me through cat-lidded eyes, cigarette dangling from her fingers, making some disdainful, probably sexual remark I don't understand.

Ilene left no suicide note, but Mom has a theory about what drove to her to it, a theory she is reluctant to share. After some coaxing, she does. Mom's theory is this: As Ilene's first marriage to the sailor unraveled, she became involved with a cop. The relationship was hot and heavy, and Ilene fell deep, being, as she was, a sucker for a man in uniform. As things progressed between them, the cop made it clear to Ilene that he loved her but didn't want kids. Shortly after, Shawn suffocated to death at home. The investigating officer was Ilene's boyfriend, who ruled the death an accident.

Mom's theory connects those pieces into something sinister. Maybe they fit together or maybe they don't. Maybe guilt over Shawn's death, accidental or otherwise, eventually led my aunt, decades after the fact, to end her life in a ratty South Florida condo. Nobody knows.

Maybe it's better if we don't.

A couple years ago, Mom handed me a slim folder containing Shawn's birth and death certificates. "This is all I have from Shawn," she explained. "I just want somebody to have it and think of him once in a while."

I've tried to do that, to occasionally offer up a little thought to the ether, not so different from the way I hit "like" on strangers' Instagram photos—just a gesture, a small something to connect when there is no other way.

My aunt's suicide has stuck with me in ways that the deaths of other, closer family members have not. I don't know why. Maybe because killing oneself seems like such a wild and unbound act. Why do some people choose to end their suffering while others, like my mom, choose to endure? Is it merely a question of feeling like you have something to live for? Or can it be flipped: Do some people feel like they have something to die for? Did my aunt feel death a more attractive option than continuing to live? What did she hope to find in death that she could not in life? The obvious answer is peace, but I wonder if that is the full answer. I suspect a fuller answer might have something to do with the desire to erase your whole being, to call a mulligan on your entire existence. To never have been.

When my aunt killed herself, I don't remember feeling horrified or sickened. I don't know what the name is for the emotion I felt, but the closest I can come is wonder, not unlike the feeling I got the first time I stood on the rim of the Grand Canyon. It wasn't so much that I thought I might jump, but that I could, and moreover, that jumping would be pretty easy.

I have certainly considered suicide. I think that's a normal thing to do. It would be hard to crawl through life's various shit piles without at least forming an opinion on the subject. My opinion is simple: Suicide seems like a reasonable solution to the intractable problem of life. I certainly don't *plan* on ending myself, but if life ever becomes too painful or awful or wearying, I remain open to the possibility. I mean, why not? We can't control all the circumstances of our lives, but we have it within us to control our deaths, and I see no reason to relinquish that option.

I have given little thought to how I would kill myself. Shooting myself in the head is out. Guns scare me and leave a mess. Hanging myself is also out because hanging somebody is a precise craft; screw it up and you're left dangling there choking and shitting your pants for long, embarrassing minutes. Throwing myself off a bridge: no. Japanese-style seppuku? Nope. I do not own a sword and none of my cooking knives are sterile. Ilene did it with pills and most likely I would do the same. Just lie down in my bed and swallow about a hundred pills of something. It doesn't matter what—a hundred of anything will almost certainly have the desired effect. Yes, overdosing seems like the best way for me to go, plus it has the added benefit that I will die doing what I love—taking pills.

To be extra clear: I don't plan on ever killing myself. For that matter, I don't plan on ever dying. But I also know that circumstances change, people change, minds change. Illness can rob the joy from life, and, as I said, Mom has already told me that if things get too bad for her, she has made what she euphemistically calls "arrangements." I don't blame her. What's better: to slip into a deep and final sleep at the time and location of one's choosing, or to expire a little later in a strange and antiseptic room lashed to machines?

Mom says she doesn't know if Ilene really meant to kill herself that day or not. She thinks maybe her sister was looking for attention, maybe trying to purge whatever demons she'd been lugging around across the years. To my knowledge, there was no funeral. No memorial service. Nothing to mark her life other than reams of unpaid bills and two boys left behind, and another already dead.

At various times while running through the wilds of Connecticut, I have seen all of our native animals: rabbits skittering across the trail, raccoons and possum and deer playing statue between the trees, hoping I have not caught sight of them, and every once in a while, an orange blur of fox disappearing into the bushes. In the springtime we have loud singing frogs looking for mates. The soprano peepers, tenor greens, baritone bullfrogs. We have field mice and snakes and Elijah said he saw a bobcat once. The other day, Martha and I were walking beside a pond. "What's this?" she said.

She bent down and picked up a hunk of bone, the skull of some small animal. We turned it over in our hands, peering into holes that used to hold eyes. It still had its sharp, meat-eating teeth. We discussed what it could have been. A raccoon, maybe, or an unlucky house cat. A tuft of gray fur hung from what used to be its chin. We put the skull back and kept walking, and that night I had bad dreams. When I woke up, it was still dark. I wrapped my arms around Martha. Everybody else was still asleep and soon I fell back to sleep, too.

CHAPTER TWENTY

See the merry widow

Martha and I both know I'm going to die before her, owing to my bad genes and her hearty Norwegian constitution. Plus, women live longer than men and righties live longer than lefties like myself. It's almost certain, therefore, that she will have many years of merry widowhood after I pass, years I already resent. "Look, there's the merry widow in her Paris flat!" "Look, there's the merry widow on a river cruise with her new beau, the haberdasher!" Ugh. The very thought of Martha's "post-me" life fills me with jealousy, which is no doubt activating the stress hormone cortisol, which, in turn, is almost certainly hastening the heart attack that will eventually kill me.

When one is married and financially solvent, it is best to have a will. I knew this but for years had put off the act of drafting one. It was just one of those unpleasant tasks I'd delayed, like the colonoscopy and every household chore Martha has ever asked me to perform. Every once in a while, Martha would say, "You know, we really should get our wills done," to which I would respond, "Absolutely," and then another year would go by where neither of us did anything about it.

After children come into the picture, wills take on even greater importance because, in addition to all the financial stuff, they dictate who will raise the kids if both parents should die. This question provoked much conflict between us. Should it be one of our brothers? Close friends? Parents? Who did we trust to give our kids as close an approximation as possible to the childhood we would have given them had we not gone down in that zeppelin disaster? After much bickering, we decided, in the event of our simultaneous deaths, to simply release the children into the wild in the hopes that a pride of lions would find them and raise them as their own.

Martha finally got fed up with my yessing her to death about getting a will and demanded we take action. Now. Yes, dear. Maybe we didn't even need a lawyer. There are websites that will draw up a will for you. I think Amazon even includes a will if you order their Prime service. But we felt uncertain about how simple or complicated the process would be, so we went with an actual living person. We asked around for a competent local lawyer, got a name, and made an appointment. The guy practiced out of an old Victorian town house that looked more like a funeral home than a law office, which I guess was appropriate, since we were there to talk about (my) death.

The lawyer sat us down at a big lawyerly-looking conference table in a big lawyerly-looking conference room, and offered us small lawyerly Dixie cups of water. He explained the process of drafting a will, which mostly entailed a series of decisions that would determine the distribution of our worldly goods, along with our choice for who would raise the kids. Interestingly, our lawyer advised us not to tell our designees that we had selected them for the job, which seemed like kind of a shitty thing to do to someone. Imagine getting a call saying your loved ones just died and—congratulations!—you're going to raise their kids. His reasoning was that, if we believe they are the right people for the job, they will do what's best by us. Telling them might only provoke arguments for a situation that is almost certainly never going to transpire.

It all seemed straightforward until he asked if we wanted to also create "living wills," which dictate what we would like done or not done in the event that either of us becomes incapacitated. This seems like a smart thing to do. Again, it's pretty straightforward: I tell the lawyer that Martha should make all of my medical decisions as my proxy. When it comes time for her to appoint me as her proxy, she hesitates.

"What's the problem?" I ask.

"I think you'll pull the plug."

Say what?

She tells the lawyer that she's afraid I will pull the plug on her at the earliest opportunity. I don't even know how to respond to this. Does she really think I'll just flip the switch off at the first sign of trouble? Like she breaks her arm and I'm like, "Better put her down."

The lawyer turns to me, eyebrows raised as if to ask, "When did you first decide to murder your wife?"

As delicately as I can, I ask Martha what the fuck she is talking about.

"I just don't trust you," she says. This is some heavy shit. How can she not trust me to do what's best for her? Haven't I done an excellent job providing for her over these last however many years? Haven't I done everything in my power to keep her safe and secure and, yes, *alive*? How many times have I accompanied her to various medical appointments? When she sliced the tip of her finger off with the kitchen knife, didn't I watch—WITH SYMPATHY—as she placed that fingertip in a sandwich baggie, and didn't I then drive her to the emergency room? Haven't I tended to her illnesses, been present for her in delivery rooms, laughed at her while she threw up after drinking too much? Never once have I slipped any medical personnel a twenty and said, "As long as we're here, why don't you end her?" I have never, ever done that, yet here I stand, accused of murder.

Probing further, I discover that Martha fears, in the event of her medical incapacitation, that I am likely to do whatever is most expedient. I assure her that I will follow her instructions to the letter. If she should fall into a coma and wants to be kept on ventilators and feeding tubes and have twice-weekly shiatsu sessions until eternity, I will make that happen. Does she want her head cut off and cryogenically frozen? I will do that.

"I don't want my head cut off."

Then I won't do that. Whatever she asks of me, I will do; that is the purpose of a living will. Meanwhile, the billable minutes are ticking away and the lawyer is watching all of this with detached amusement on his face, perhaps wondering which of us he will represent in the divorce.

Eventually, and after much cajoling, she does agree to let me serve as her medical proxy but only because she cannot think of anybody better, and only after wringing multiple promises from me that I will not kill her. I promise and promise and promise, but who are we kidding? I probably will.

The rest of the document is pretty straightforward: I get her stuff, she gets my stuff, the kids get our stuff. Fortunately, I have not found the level of professional success that would prompt a big fight over my estate, so the kids will most likely inherit not much more than some decent furniture and a sizable collection of cassettes.

Once we finally sign and notarize our wills, Martha asks how I feel. I tell her I found the experience of talking through the details of our deaths to be mildly discomfiting, especially in front of a lawyer who admitted, when I asked, that the bookshelf behind him filled with legal tomes was "mostly for show."

(Apparently, everything is online now, so he doesn't need books, but he feels that clients like to see the law library so he keeps it around.)

"But aren't you glad we finally did it?"

"Not really," I answer. Completing my will felt tantamount to signing my own death sentence. Yes, I know I'm going to die one day, but I didn't like making it official. If something isn't official, maybe it won't happen. I'd had the same reaction when I took out a life insurance policy a few years before.

Getting life insurance is less ghoulish than writing a will, because it's simply a hedge in the *unlikely* event of my death. That's the key word: *unlikely*. After all, the life insurance company is betting that I'm *not* going to die. People not dying is how they make their money. If everybody who took out life insurance expired before their policies did, they'd be out of business. The fact that insurance companies are profitable corporate entities who are rich enough to buy blimps to fly over sporting events leads me to believe that *they* believe I will *not* die. Viewed in this way, buying a life insurance policy is actually a great way to guarantee I'll live, because I have never outwitted a corporation and doubt I ever will.

Determining the correct amount of life insurance to purchase was the tricky part. I knew firsthand the value of the stuff, since it was life insurance that kept my siblings and me afloat in the years after Dad died. He'd had the foresight to take out a robust policy that kept us fed, clothed, and educated until we reached adulthood. So I knew I needed to insure myself for a sizable enough amount that my family would be taken care of in the event of my early demise, but I didn't want to take out a large enough policy to give anybody a motive. In the end, I insured myself for enough that, should I die, Martha and the kids will have enough money to hold on to the house and feed themselves, but not enough money to keep the lights on. That way, it's in both of our interests that I stay alive, because I like to live and she likes electricity.

An interesting side note: Until recently, I believed that a life insurance policy wouldn't pay off if you commit suicide, but a friend of mine said he'd done some research into the matter during a prolonged stretch of financial misfortune in his own life and discovered that they actually will pay off if you've had the policy for over two years. Great news if I decide to kill myself, as I have already said I might. Not likely, but possible. As for my friend, he jumped off a bridge.

"I would never kill myself," Martha says. Good. That's good. While I reserve the right to take my own life one day, she is not allowed. Nobody I love is ever allowed to kill themselves. That probably seems hypocritical, but as I have often said, I am fine with hypocrisy so long as the hypocrite is me.

A weird game to play is to mentally assemble any group of people and try to guess which of them will die first. In my group, the group of Martha and the kids and me, it will be me. That's okay. One of the surprising things I've learned since starting a family is that I am capable of valuing other people's lives more than my own.

The kids will live a long time. Martha is going to live a long time, too. That's not speculation on my part. It's fact. As part of obtaining life insurance, Martha and I both had to get physicals and submit to blood tests. Mine came back normal. When hers came back, our insurer told her she had the cholesterol and heart rate of an elite athlete. "You can eat bacon and eggs every day for the rest of your life and not have to worry," he told her. Plus, she's got a gaggle of crusty old ladies in her gene pool, so she should be fine.

See the merry widow playing tennis with her new friend the handsome schoolmaster. The merry widow building housing for orphans in Guatemala. The merry widow sampling local wiener schnitzel at a café on the Danube. The merry widow, old and happy, wrapped in a shawl, sitting at the kitchen table in winter, thinking of her late husband who died much too young and much too handsome but who had the foresight to draft a will and get life insurance. "Good man," thinks the merry widow. "Good man."

CHAPTER TWENTY-ONE

"She's a nice lady"

Mom's on oxygen now. Whatever metric they use to check her oxygen levels isn't supposed to fall below 70 percent. Well, Mom's levels now fall below that, so they've given her supplemental oxygen she wheels around in a little tank. Combine that with her three-wheeled motorized scooter, and Mom now needs five wheels to move through her day. If she gets any more, she'll require a trucker's license to leave the house.

She doesn't have to use the oxygen all the time yet, but she needs it more than they initially thought she would. Her spirits remain good, but I know that each new indignity—the scooter, the oxygen, the colostomy bag—feels like another step closer to the end. Before, when she told me she felt like she'd wasted her life, I didn't ask the obvious question. So I ask now.

"What did you want to do?"

"I really wanted to go to law school. I had very good grades, but my guidance counselor talked me out of it because he said girls can't be lawyers. He said, 'You can be a teacher or a secretary or something.' And I was too young and stupid to buck the system."

Mom made up for her lack of system bucking in later years, first by coming out as a lesbian when doing so meant to risk being ostracized or worse. She sued the state of Illinois to provide better services for Susan and children like Susan, a case she won. Later, she sued the state of New Jersey to force them to offer better educational opportunities for Susan and children like Susan. She won that case, too. With Elaine, she fought for the Equal Rights Amendment. She ran for the local school board but lost. Growing up, it seemed to me that we were forever bucking the system, and all that effort— the effort of trying to live as a blended gay family under dubious financial and psychological circumstances—exacted a severe toll on everybody. Bucking the system seemed to cost us all a great deal.

Her other regret, she says, is the way she raised us. "I'm not happy with the parenting job I did. At all."

I know what she means, but I don't make her say it. Nor do I contradict her. The fact is, she's right. Or, in my view, half right. As a parent now myself, I feel I have two responsibilities. The first is to make sure my kids know they are loved, and I can find no fault with Mom in that regard. As I said earlier, she always let us know she loved us. The second is to make kids feel safe. And in that, she failed.

Our household felt stuffed with danger, the way an olive is stuffed with a pimiento, bright and red and in the center of everything. Nobody could ever relax there, because any little thing could set off either Elaine or Mom. Maybe one of us had failed to "properly" vacuum the dog hair from the stairs or left the toilet seat up or not come running at the sound of our name being called. Maybe somebody had left dirty dishes in the sink or eaten the Entenmann's chocolate chip cookies without permission. Maybe nobody had done anything.

Once I received detention in school for something and had to have Mom sign a pink form acknowledging that she knew I'd been punished. Rather than face her wrath, I forged her name on the form and stuffed it into a clear plastic pencil pouch in my three-ring binder. Mom found the slip. After the screaming subsided ("Liar!" "Sneak!"

"Bastard!"), she tacked a long list of chores to the kitchen bulletin board for me to complete as punishment. At the bottom of that list, I wrote "Heil Hitler," not a smart move in a Jewish household. More rage and punishment followed—in fairness, that one's on me.

But she was right, in a way. I did lie. I did sneak around. Not because I had anything in particular to hide, but because I always felt so on edge, so terrified that I would be called to task for one offense or another. Elaine's son bore the worst of it. Elaine routinely terrified him, beating him with her words, calling him worthless, fat, stupid. If Mom tried to step in, Elaine turned her fury on her, screaming at Mom to stay the hell out of her business and away from her son. Eventually, Mom stopped defending him. Nobody defended him. He moved away after high school and even though I grew up with him, I haven't seen him since.

Living like that, day after day, wears on you. The constant stress fills the house with a kind of smog. The air itself feels toxic. Sometimes you carry it with you, as I did, for years. Sometimes you never leave it behind.

I ask Mom about her own mother, Grandma CeCe, short for Cecile. "Oh, she was horrible," says Mom. "Horrible."

In her adult life, Mom created an environment that almost perfectly matched the one in which she grew up. Like her mother, Mom had three kids, the youngest with serious medical problems. My mother's brother, my uncle, was born with a serious kidney ailment that required frequent hospitalization and a tremendous amount of money, money my grandfather struggled to earn. Grandpa traveled a lot for work, leaving Grandma home to raise three kids and take care of her own mother, who lived with them. Grandma did not possess the coping mechanisms to deal. Mom says, "I think she was so tired that anything that happened, she would take a negative attitude toward, and yell and scream and hit."

"I didn't realize she was a hitter," I say.

"Oh, she was lovely," Mom replies.

The turmoil in their childhood household strikes me as being a lot like the turmoil I experienced. I ask her about the parallels between the two households. Was our house like the house in which she grew up?

"It was. Yes, it was. I knew it and I didn't know how to correct it. I was afraid of Elaine like I was afraid of my mother. It was bad. It was just bad."

"Did Elaine ever hit you?" I ask.

"Yes."

I never knew that.

We sit in silence for a moment or two before she speaks again. "Now that you've gotten me nauseous and I could throw up, do you have any nicer questions?"

Not really, no.

We hang up and I start thinking about my own relationship with Grandma. I'd never been very close with her. She lived too far away, in Chicago, and the couple of times a year we saw her, she yelled a lot. At store clerks and waiters and people on the sidewalk and people who displeased her, which seemed to be everybody. The whole world had in for Grandma, and she let the whole world know she wasn't going to take it. Mom thinks CeCe was a much better grandparent than parent, but I didn't see much evidence of that.

After Dad died, Mom sent Eric and me to Chicago to stay with Grandma CeCe for a couple weeks. I'm not sure what Mom thought that would accomplish, other than to get us out of our surroundings for a little while to clear our heads. Grandma's apartment was small and deadly boring in the way that all adult homes seem to kids. There was literally nothing for us to do, other than sit in her cramped living room and watch *All My Children* with her every afternoon, a program Grandma attended to with religious fervor. To those who belittle soap operas, I say this: Watch one every day for two weeks and see if you, too, don't find it the most compelling form of entertainment yet created.

One day, Grandma offered to take us to a movie of our choice. Eric and I selected *Purple Rain*, which had just come out. I don't know why we picked it, other than the fact that Prince rode a purple motorcycle on the poster. For those unfamiliar, *Purple Rain* is Prince's cinematic autobiography, heavy on funky rock music and just as heavy on sex. Dirty sex. I have never felt more uncomfortable than while watching that four-and-a-half-foot-tall purple-garbed sex god get freaky in front of my grandmother, a woman who bore three children but who, I am confident, never had intercourse. Nobody had much to say about the movie afterward, because it's hard to have a conversation with your grandmother about Apollonia's perfect, cinnamon-colored nipples.

Sometime near the end of our stay, Eric and I were parked in our preferred position in front of the television when Grandma came out of her room, a basket of laundry on her hip, and unloaded on us:

"Why am I doing everything around here? You two don't do anything except sit there. You're spoiled and ungrateful!"

I remember my shock at her outburst. What did she mean spoiled and ungrateful? Didn't she know my father had just died and I was excused from all chores for the rest of my life? That's the way the death of a parent works: A parent dies and the child is allowed to do whatever he or she wants, forever. Not that I felt I was putting one over on Grandma—I mean, what was I supposed to be doing that I wasn't doing? The laundry? I didn't know how to do laundry. Moms do laundry, and if not moms, grandmoms. That's just the way it is. How did she not know this?

Grandma stormed out of the apartment, leaving me and Eric to regard each other in shocked silence. We hadn't thought we were being assholes, but Grandma put us straight. Assholes we were, spoiled and ungrateful. At the moment, I don't think either of us felt we had much to be grateful *for*, but that was probably just further evidence of our ingratitude. If Mom's plan in sending us to Chicago was to make us feel better, it didn't work.

Grandma's infrequent visits to New Jersey provoked in me a small dread. It wasn't that I didn't like being around her exactly, but I didn't know what it was I was supposed to do with a grandmother. What good was she? She didn't play, wasn't funny, didn't spoil us. It wasn't even clear that she liked us very much. If anything, interactions with Grandma felt forced, with me trying to occupy our empty conversational space with the same filler I used in the obligatory thank-you cards Mom made me write for the five-dollar bills she sent on our birthdays.

"Dear Grandma, Thank you for the five-dollar bill you sent for my birthday." Then I would stare at my stationery for long minutes, pencil gripped in hand, trying to conjure up something more to write. Maybe something about my daily triumphs and struggles: "School is good." Perfect. What next? Something relatable, maybe, perhaps about the weather? "The weather is hot." Yeah, good: pithy and descriptive. More, more. Any recent activities? "I went to a Yankees game last week with my friend." Great, now to bring this missive to a close with a white lie and a fake sign of affection. "I hope I get to see you soon. Love, Michael."

I was living in New York when I got the call that Grandma had died. Just after her eightieth birthday. A couple of years before, with her health in decline, she had moved to Florida to be near Mom. After a lifetime of snowy Chicago winters, I don't think Grandma ever felt at home among the palm trees and strip malls. She didn't belong there. Didn't make friends at her apartment complex. I don't know where she belonged. The conversation with Mom was short and to the point. "Grandma died," she said. No, she didn't want me to come down there. "There won't be a funeral," she said.

Martha only met her once, in Florida. The three of us had ice cream together, three small cups of vanilla soft-serve. This was toward the end of her life, when her walk had slowed and she had mellowed. She took my arm from the car to the ice cream place. I don't think she feared falling; I think she just liked holding my arm. I remember sitting at an outdoor patio table filling the conversation with the same fluff I always had, wishing I felt closer to her but not knowing how. I remember a moment when I caught Grandma's eye scrutinizing me; it was just a moment, but I think I saw her feeling happy for me. And I think feeling happy for me made her happy, too. Grandma was kind to Martha, asking her about her childhood in Minnesota, her parents, her brother and sister. We ate our ice cream and Grandma held my arm again as we walked back to the car and up to her apartment, still deadly boring. Afterward, when Martha and I were alone and quiet together, Martha said, "She's a nice lady."

One of the few things about which I feel I've gained any wisdom as I've grown older is the insight that nearly everybody believes himself to be a good person. We all feel as though we're doing our best. When others find us obnoxious or insolent or cruel, it is only, we think, because we were misunderstood or because they deserved it, or because they are the bad people. Not us. Nobody thinks of himself as a villain. Not even villains.

Elaine was doing her best, Mom hers. Grandma, I'm sure, was doing her best, too. In my daily life, I've made a conscious effort to try to meet people where they are, to see them as I see myself, imperfect but trying. Sometimes it's easier than others. Sometimes it's hardest with the people I love. My patience with strangers is often greater than it is with my wife and children. Why is that? Maybe because we are unafraid to show our worst selves to the people who share our homes. That seems backward to me, because those who have chosen to love us deserve the best we have to offer, and also because the people we live with know where we keep the knives.

CHAPTER TWENTY-TWO

"Well, that's my story"

My list of dead family members keeps growing, as these lists have a tendency to do over time. Grandpa Sam and cousin Shawn. Then, when I was five, my paternal grandmother, Bernice. I remember the morning after her death, seeing Dad's long face, haggard as he took the stairs one at a time down to breakfast. Mom told us to behave extra well that day, and we did. Then Dad died. Aunt Ilene. Grandma CeCe. Grandpa Leon, the cop I never knew. An ancient aunt who kept a windup canary in a cage. A long-lost uncle who died without a will.

Yesterday I caught myself plucking a white hair from my temple. I lassoed it around my pointer finger and tugged, holding it up to the light for inspection. White from stem to stern. I don't think I had white hair like that when I started writing this book two years ago. My body is different now. The wedding photos on my bedroom wall show a different body still. None of these bodies resembles Bruce Whitehall.

Often before showering, I stare at my whole self in the mirror. There it is, the whole lousy sum of me: legs and paunch and ribs and shoulders laced with red slashes from sleep scratching, flaccid penis hanging down like an aardvark snout. I don't know why I do this. It's a compulsion, I guess, like if I look hard enough, I'll discover the real me, the secret me I've been hiding from myself all these years. Like, "Ta da! There you are!" But the mirror disappoints again and again. What am I hoping I will find if I look long enough? Whose face do I think will emerge?

Here's a story I've never told anybody. When I was about ten or eleven years old, Elaine mentioned that a friend's sister had taken ill. Gravely ill. Heart problems, maybe. Kidney? I don't recall, but I remember Elaine saying the doctors weren't sure if she would make it through the night. It was a woman I barely knew, but it scared me to think that somebody I had a passing acquaintance with could be dead by morning.

After dinner I went up to my room and locked myself in the bathroom. I began praying, although the prayer I issued seemed unlike any I'd heard before. Instead of communicating with God, I was trying to reach out directly through space to the woman in the hospital. I tried picturing her lying in a hospital bed, stretching my thoughts out to her as I repeated, "You're going to be okay. You're going to be okay." Over and over. "A hundred percent better," I whispered. I stared into the mirror, deep into the black of my pupils, repeating these chants dozens, maybe hundreds, of times. "You're going to be okay. A hundred percent better." I don't know how long I stayed in there. Maybe half an hour. Maybe longer. When I felt I had done all I could do, I left the bathroom and went to bed.

The next night at dinner, I asked about the woman. Elaine brightened. "Can you believe it? She's out of the hospital. She says she feels a hundred percent better." When I heard that phrase—"a hundred percent better"—I knew. My message had been received.

What do you make of a story like that? It bothered me for a long, long time because I could not discount the experience, nor did I wish to make more of it than it was. Maybe it was nothing. But maybe it was, and if it was, it scared me. The praytheist mind can only find so many coincidences in this life before turning on itself. I'm not ready to accept God, not yet, probably not ever, but I like that He keeps reminding me to not give up looking for Him.

Sometimes after I turn on the shower and I'm waiting for the water to heat up, I stare deep into the black of my own eyes and try to connect with whatever force I thought I felt when I was a ten-year-old compelled to reach out to a woman I barely knew. It was as intense a feeling as I've ever felt, an almost electrical connection I believed myself to be putting out into the world. The kind of thing only a kid could believe.

There's something wrong with Martha's lungs. Over the last couple of years, she keeps getting recurrent bouts of pneumonia. Two or three times a year. She takes antibiotics, which knock it out after a few days, but it keeps returning. Finally, a pulmonologist diagnosed bronchiectasis, a condition that damages the airways to the lungs. As a result, mucus builds up and collects in the lungs, and thus: pneumonia. The doctor put her on a mucus thinner and told her to drink a lot of water. Beyond that there's not much they can do other than continue to give her antibiotics when it flares up. There's no cure for bronchiectasis, but as long as we keep our eyes on it she should be okay. She worries about the progressive inflammation in her lungs one day causing cancer. But it won't. It can't, because her life insurance policy is considerably smaller than mine. And also because it just can't.

Sometimes she says to me, "Can you believe we've known each other twenty years?"

Sometimes as we kiss when I'm leaving the house she tells me to wear my seat belt even though she knows I always wear my seat belt.

Sometimes I remember Elijah, age two or three, naked but for a diaper, waddling across the grass. We'd just moved to a new house and we had a big side lawn, a vast expanse of green leading to the woods. I stood quite a ways back from him watching him go, fat little legs propelling him toward some distant destination he alone held in his head. I remember thinking he would always be walking away from us like that, and that I had to learn to be okay with that. Now he's fourteen and I'm still not okay with it.

I've got a scrap of yellow notebook paper in my desk drawer that has the address of the cemetery where Dad is buried. I've only been there once. I keep meaning to go back. Eric and I have talked about going together, but we haven't done it yet. Maybe this spring when the weather turns. It's not too far. We could get sandwiches, make a day of it.

Yesterday I reminded Mom about the second time she heard the Voice, the one she first heard before tumor surgery. Did she remember yet what it said when she heard it again?

"No," she said. "Sandy and I have discussed it a few times. I cannot remember."

I'm exasperated. Does she remember anything about it?

"I have a feeling that I was in the mountains. . . . We were driving through the Pisgah National Forest, beautiful sunny day. We had a tape of beautiful Jewish music we loved to hear . . . and, like, this peace or something came over me. . . ." She pauses, then continues. "My God was right there."

I think she means somebody or some force reached out to be with her, just the way I tried to reach out to that woman I barely knew lying in a hospital bed all those years ago. Maybe that's all God is, energy reaching out to itself at the places where it needs a little help. Mom and I sit with that for a second; then I say, "All right, I have nothing else to say to you today."

She laughs. We chitchat for a couple minutes more about the grandchildren. She forgot to call Elijah on his birthday and feels terrible. I assure her it's okay. He knows she loves him. She tells him all the time. After a few minutes more, I know she's ready to end the conversation, because she always says the same thing when she's ready to get off the phone: "Well, that's my story."

"Enjoy your Sunday," I tell her.

"Love you, Mikey."

"Love you, too, Mom."

I hang up. It's March here in the wilds of Connecticut. We've had a lot of snow the past few weeks. It's piled in high drifts, and from my office window, I can see deep into the trees. I look for animal tracks in the snow but see none. I stand and stretch and straighten out my scoliosis shoulder. I roll my head around my neck, my joints cracking like popping corn. I do a quick inventory of my family. Everybody is where they should be: here, safe and warm. Elijah is on the computer playing Minecraft. Ruthie is in her room gabbing to one of her friends on the iPad I told her I would not buy her but did anyway. Martha reads the Sunday *Times* in the living room, a blanket Santa brought tucked around her waist. I head upstairs and throw on some sweats and a long-sleeve technical shirt and my puffy black vest. I come back downstairs, call the dog.

"Ole Ole Ole!" I yodel. He lifts himself from the floor and trots over to me. I grab his leash, loop it over his neck.

"Where are you going?" Martha asks. I have to ask her to repeat it because I honestly cannot hear. "WHERE ARE YOU GOING?"

"I'm going to head over to the park with Ole."

"It's snowy out there. Be careful."

I tell her I will be. I struggle into my boots and open the front door and step outside into the cold, clean air. It's a good day to run.

Addendum

On April 8, 2015, I scheduled a colonoscopy.

On April 9, 2015, I joined a gym.

Author's Note

All the events in this book are true to the best of my recollection. Undoubtedly, I got some things wrong, but I don't know which things and you don't either, so let's both pretend everything happened exactly the way I said it did. Also, my memory is not good enough to remember actual conversations I have had in the past. That should be obvious to anybody with a memory. Most of the dialogue in this book is fabricated but represents actual conversations I have had, with words I would have used. I have done this to the best of my ability, with all the usual caveats, including the caveat of my having a less-than-optimal Neanderthal brain.

On the other hand, all present-day dialogue with my mother is genuine and verbatim. Over the course of writing this book, I conducted several interviews with her, and all of our dialogue is transcribed from those discussions. Some of it has been condensed or slightly edited for clarification, but that's it. An example of condensing is when she had to interrupt our conversation to yell at her stupid dog, Jake. This happened many times because the dog is very stupid.

Finally, I changed several names to protect the identities of people. This is a smart thing to do when identifying somebody as a "rage addict," or when discussing somebody's involvement with a certain criminal enterprise known for murdering people who reveal too much about its business or members.

Acknowledgments

For advice and help and general encouragement, thank you to: Abby Zidle, Tricia Boczkowski, Polly Watson, everybody at Gallery Books, Barry Goldblatt, Jane Goldberg, Mary Kobayashi, and Paget Brewster.

Thank you, of course, to my wife, Martha, and children, Elijah and Ruthie, who do not mind when I tease them but like it best when I tease myself.

And special thanks to my mother, Jill Schwartz, who shared with me intimate details of her life without asking for anything in return other than a substantial share of book profits. I neglected to tell her that my books don't have profits. She is going to be very disappointed.